THE HUNTED

"People in my profession," he said, "we trade information. It's like a currency sometimes, even more valuable than money. I was trying to settle a case on Bellerophon, one corporation suing another over breach of contract, when I heard about them."

"The Predators," said Andar.

The lawyer wiped his forehead with a tattered sleeve, smearing the dirt that had collected during his flight through the forest, and said, "Yes. The Predators. EarthGov has been keeping them a secret until now, and for good reason. They're not human. They're another species altogether."

"Aliens . . . ?" said Mara disbelievingly.

"They're a race of hunters, and they have been using Earth as a hunting ground for centuries. Maybe millennia. No one is certain."

"What are they after?" asked Sildar.

Broadhurst looked up at him. "Sport, apparently. They get their kicks out of tracking us down and killing us, much as we used to get our kicks out of hunting game."

"Wait a minute," said Abelkis. "We're not game. We're *people.*"

Other Predator novels from Dark Horse Books

PREDATOR™
FLESH AND BLOOD

a novel by

MICHAEL JAN FRIEDMAN
and
ROBERT GREENBERGER

*Based on the motion picture
from Twentieth Century Fox*

DARK HORSE BOOKS®
Milwaukie

Book design by Debra Bailey
Cover painting by Stephen Youll

Published by Dark Horse Books
A division of Dark Horse Comics
10956 SE Main Street
Milwaukie, OR 97222

darkhorse.com

First Dark Horse Books Edition: September 2007
ISBN: 978-1-59582-047-1

Printed in USA

10 9 8 7 6 5 4 3 2 1

ONE

"You know, it's funny," said Andar Ciejek, gazing at the screen suspended from a tensor arm in the ceiling of the cramped, little comm compartment.

The screen showed him Katarina's heart-shaped face framed in cascades of dark, flowing hair. Her eyes were dark as well, and big. And full of concern, as much as she tried to conceal it.

"What is?" she asked, her voice a melody.

Andar loved that about her—the way her voice was like music. That and everything else.

"I don't remember much about my grandfather," he told her.

They hadn't ever talked about the old man. But then, he had never had any reason to bring up that subject.

Katarina tilted her head. "I thought you lived with him."

"We lived in the same compound. He was big on keeping his family close by. Still, I didn't see much of him. Just on holidays and birthdays. And funerals, of course. There always seemed to be a lot of those."

"Your grandfather was a busy man," said Katarina, with only a hint of irony in her voice.

Andar frowned. Karl Ciejek had been busy all right. But it wasn't until Andar became a teenager that he realized *how* busy, or with what kind of enterprises. It still irked him that his father, Gregor, hadn't seen fit to discuss the family business with him as he was growing up—that he had been forced to figure it out on his own, putting together the grim news items on the web with the offhand snippets of information he picked up at mealtime or around the family pool.

He remembered all too vividly the pushing match that had ensued with his father, and the bitter words, and the feeling that he had been betrayed. He had grown up believing his relatives were loving, generous people, esteemed by those who worked for them as well as the galaxy at large. It turned out to be far from the truth.

The Ciejeks were carrion eaters, feeding off the diseased, overpopulated carcass that remained of Mother Earth. They smuggled, skimmed, strong-armed, and exploited every last possible human misery to make their blood money. And when they had to, they used ruthless force to crush the competition—or blunt the eagerness of some public prosecutor seeking to make a name for himself.

Andar had promised himself that he would leave the family compound at his first opportunity and never look back. On his twenty-first birthday, he did as he had vowed. He headed for Earth, of all places, rather than one of her myriad colonies, and took a job in a domed city with a well-meaning but poorly run ozone-restoration company.

That was where he met Katarina. She was one of the pilots who released the ozone packets into the stratosphere. It didn't take long for Andar to fall in love with her, or for the company to fall in love with *him*.

If not for Katarina, he would likely have gone to a more efficient outfit. There were plenty of them, Earth's stratosphere being what it was. But he stayed, and helped the company remain afloat, and in time grew too enamored of his colleagues to consider leaving—despite the offers that seemed to arrive every other month.

He had Katarina and a comfortable job and a little recognition. What else did he need? Not perks—but he got them anyway. It was one of the ways his employers showed their

gratitude. The biggest one was the annual terraforming confer-
ence in the Atheneum on Mars.

His coworkers would have killed to attend. Andar, on the
other hand, would happily have skipped it. But Katarina urged
him to go. She said it would give him a broader perspective on
the work they did.

So he packed his bags and said goodbye to her, his expectation being that he would see her again in a couple of weeks. He
could manage that, if only barely. Then came the news of his
grandfather's death.

No one in the family could have expected Andar to make
the funeral. There were too many jumps involved for him to
get there in time. But his presence was required for the reading
of the will.

Andar's first thought was to throw away whatever his
grandfather had left him and let the rest of the family fight
over it. After all, he had left the compound for a reason.
Then he remembered all the people who had worked for his
father.

When Gregor Ciejek died three years ago, his employees'
contracts had been picked up by Andar's grandfather. It was
the honorable thing to do. And as much as Gregor and Karl
had bickered, the old man loved his eldest son. He would never
have allowed Gregor's people to go unsheltered.

Besides, they knew too much. And there were those in the
sector who would have given a fortune—maybe two—to get
the inside scoop on the Ciejek family's operations. So Karl had
kept Gregor's people on, finding work for them to do, treating
them as his own.

But now Karl was as dead as his son, and Gregor's people
had no one to look after them. They had made a lot of
enemies working for Gregor, and even more of them working
for Karl. It would be bad for them, very bad, unless Andar
stepped in.

Just for a little while. Long enough to make sure they weren't left high and dry. Then he would leave again.

Andar wished there were a way to do this long-distance. If he were a member of some other family, it wouldn't have been a problem. But if he had belonged to some other family, he probably wouldn't have bolted in the first place.

"You still there?" Katarina asked.

He re-focused on her. She was starting to get fuzzy—the product of his increasing distance from Earth. He was already well past the last EarthGov signal booster. They had a few minutes, he estimated, five if they were lucky.

"Yes," he confirmed. "Still here."

"How long until you reach Felicity?"

A hot, smelly jungle world that the Ciejeks had riddled with precious-metal mines. In fact, there was nothing felicitous about it. Then again, the trend these days was to name planets ironically.

"Five days," he said. "Five *long* days."

"They wouldn't seem so long if I were with you. But you nixed that idea."

"Trust me, leaving you on Earth was the nicest thing I could ever have done. Felicity isn't exactly a paradise. And my family . . . well . . ."

Katarina had taken the news of his background well, when he finally got up the courage to share it with her. He had left his relatives, after all. He wasn't any more a part of them than she was.

"I know. But I could have watched your back—especially when your cousin Derek is around."

Andar's stomach muscles tightened at the thought of his cousin—his uncle's sloppy fat son, older than Andar by a couple of years. As a kid, Derek had gotten his kicks dismembering insects. Later on, he had turned to raping the servants. And no one had ever taken him to task for it.

Except Andar. He had caught Derek trying to have his way with the daughter of one of Gregor Ciejek's bodyguards. It had taken a long time for the swelling to go down so Derek could see out of that eye again.

Unfortunately, Derek—as Karl Ciejek's other grandson, and the one who had remained with the family—would be getting the lion's share of the inheritance. Andar was pretty certain of that. But as far as he was concerned, the fat boy could have it. Andar just wanted to make sure Derek didn't pull anyone's legs off.

Suddenly, Katarina's image fritzed on the screen. "I'm losing you," he told her.

"Not likely," she said. "Take care of yourself, all right? I want you back in one piece."

"That's my hope, too."

But he wasn't sure she heard him, because he could barely see her anymore for all the static zagging across the screen. Five minutes had been a gross overestimation. They had barely had *one*.

"Katarina?" he said.

No response. And a few moments later, her image was lost in the garble of interference. Reluctantly, Andar deactivated the comm receiver. The screen on the end of the tensor arm went black, offering him a reflection of his own head and shoulders.

He took note of the two days' growth of beard that blurred the sharp, lean lines of his face. His hair was light-colored like his mother's, whom he had lost when he was still a baby. A horrible ground-vehicle accident—though given his family history, the accident might have been something else.

The only feature he had inherited from his father—and his grandfather—was the cleft in his chin. He had often considered removing it, but for one reason or another hadn't gotten around to it. Maybe seeing his relatives would disgust him enough to prompt him to have the surgery.

Except Katarina sort of liked it. So then again, maybe not.

"Andar?" called a man's voice, made tinny by the ship's second-rate intercom system. But then, Owen Broadhurst's voice was tinny to begin with. "If you're finished, you might want to get out of there. It's costing you a mint."

Always watching the money, Andar thought. Just as his father had wanted.

Broadhurst, Gregor's lawyer and now Andar's by default, was the one who had called with the news of Karl's demise. He was also the one who had arranged for Andar's passage to Felicity, and rendezvoused with him at Polyphemus for the last leg of his journey. It wasn't just to renew old acquaintances. There were things to discuss before Andar was reunited with his family.

Especially my cousin Derek. His stomach lurched at the thought.

Light reflected off the gleaming steel blade as it flew through the air, end over end. With a loud thunk, it sunk deep into the two-meter-tall target at one end of the metal compartment. The hunter Bet-Karh didn't pause to appreciate his accuracy— the sound was enough for him to know he had struck home. With practiced ease, he flexed his legs and sprang high into the air, simultaneously releasing another blade. This time, it was in the opposite direction. The result—and the sound— was the same.

Landing on the balls of his feet, he crouched—and listened. He could hear the air circulating through the filters, relays snapping in response to command impulses, deck plates creaking under the stress of interstellar travel. But the sound he chose to focus on was the in and out of his breath. He used it to calm himself, to prepare . . .

Skang!

Twisting to avoid the beam of red light that suddenly slashed the room in half, he brought his right arm across his body and fired from his shoulder-mounted plasma weapon. The target this time was smaller, barely a meter tall, but wide and squat—simulating an inhabitant of a world with heavy gravity.

Names of planets didn't interest Bet-Karh. Only their inhabitants . . . his *prey*. The shot was true and the target's midsection vanished in a burst of flame and a puff of smoke. Pretty much all that remained was the head, which, if he were facing a real adversary and not an inanimate one, would barely have been worthy of a place in his trophy collection.

A dull chime sounded, ending the hunter's practice session. He took a cleansing breath and allowed himself a moment to survey the training room. Cubs would come in soon and clear out the mess as part of their daily chores. They would study the wreckage, wondering at his quickness and efficiency and wishing they were like him.

No one trained aboard the ship as hard or as often as he did. No one lived more for the Hunt. All he desired in his life were challenges worthy of the skills he had honed to perfection. Let the others fight for their perches in the clan hierarchy; it mattered little to him. The Hunt was everything.

Besides, the last thing the clan needed was another voice in the roiling cauldron of discord. His brethren navigated their way through disagreement after disagreement as if they thrived on them. The situation had gone on for a long time, and it promised to go on longer still.

In most cases, such disharmony would have ended with a battle to the death, leaving a single voice to lead the clan. But not in this instance. They couldn't afford to weaken themselves by killing each other.

The hunter made a clicking sound with his mandibles. It was an expression of disgust, from the depths of his belly. Unfortunately, he could let it out only in the privacy of the training room.

It had been a desperate move to try to forge a new clan from the remains of two others. But what choice did they have—any of them? Neither clan on its own had been numerous enough to defend itself. Both of them had skirted the abyss, looking down into the depths of extinction. They had felt the glare of their respective ancestors, whose names would be lost without mouths to speak them.

Together, as one clan, they at least had a chance. Bet-Karh would do nothing to jeopardize it.

Celina Laban, the late Gregor Ciejek's chief of operations, sat in her cabin on the passenger transport *Skidbladnir* and lifted a steaming mug of coffee to her lips. She paused, inhaling the rich, dusky aroma. It was real coffee from real beans, not the artificial stuff peddled in sector markets from one end of space to the other. Having managed a significant portion of Ciejek family operations these last eight years, Laban had gotten accustomed to the finer things in life.

She had grown up a military brat, both her father and her mother serving as officers at the Inner System Training Base. It was a Spartan existence, made even more so by her parents' obsession with saving their creds—a habit that might have stood them in good stead if their favorite bank hadn't gone belly up, sucked dry by a greedy administrator. Celina had vowed to herself that she would know the luxuries her parents hadn't—that she would wash the dust of a dozen moons out of her throat with something old and fine and expensive.

And she had.

There were those who hadn't believed she was strong enough to carry on Gregor's operations without him. They had learned otherwise. The fact was that she was even stronger than her former employer—stronger than *anyone*.

Except maybe Karl Ciejek, the patriarch of the family. But he wasn't exactly in the running anymore.

Closing her eyes, Laban savored the taste of the coffee. Then she put down the mug and considered the computer screen in front of her. Andar Ciejek's image was spread across it from one end to the other. It was a picture of him taken when he was a teenager, before the rift opened between him and his father.

He was tanned, smiling, his chin sporting his first fuzzy hint of a beard. Gregor stood behind him, his muscular arm draped over the boy's chest, his fingers locked around Andar's shoulder. Gregor had loved him—there was no question about it. That was why, right or wrong, he had tried to protect Andar from the truth about the Ciejeks.

But Andar wasn't a boy anymore. And in a way he was no longer a member of the family. That made him something of a puzzle, and Laban didn't like puzzles.

To that point, Andar had refused the creds she sent him, first at Gregor's behest and later as a condition of his will. But Gregor's fortune was small potatoes compared to Karl's. That fact alone might be enough to turn Andar around.

He wouldn't be the first fish to turn down a modest piece of bait and snap like crazy at a generous one. There were degrees of greed. Everyone had his price.

And if Andar was on his way to Felicity to snap at the bait? What would happen to *her*? Would her responsibilities grow— or diminish? Or would she be relieved of them altogether?

Laban was brought out of her introspection by the buzzing of the door. Tapping at the keyboard in front of her, she called up a gray and green graphic in the corner of her screen. It showed her the identities of the three men requesting to see her.

They were later than expected. *Again*. And they knew how much she liked her employees to be on time.

"Come in," she said in her soft, throaty voice—the one she had practiced since she was a little girl.

Then she swiveled in her chair and watched her three visitors enter the room. LeFleur, the hulking, baldheaded man standing guard in the corridor outside, didn't greet any of them. But then, LeFleur was originally one of Gregor's men.

The others Laban had brought with her when she arrived at the family compound on Minos.

It wasn't that LeFleur had ever given her reason to think him untrustworthy. *Quite the contrary,* she reflected. But she trusted her own men more.

"What have you got?" she asked them, without preamble.

The shortest of the three, a stocky, red-haired specimen with pale skin and thick, freckled hands, made a point of taking a seat before he spoke. "And how was *your* morning?" he asked in a cultured voice.

Laban didn't answer.

The red-haired man—whose name was Mara—laughed softly. "What we've got," he said, "is a young woman, one Katarina Santodonato. Twenty-six years old, father deceased, mother lives on Prosperity, no sisters or brothers. She and Andar are all but engaged."

Laban nodded. "How did they meet?'

"They work together on Earth," said Mara. "That ozone restoration outfit . . ."

"I remember," said Laban. "Anything else?"

"Not yet," he said.

"Keep at it." The girl might prove important as leverage. Not that Laban was eager to blackmail Andar, but she would do it if the situation warranted.

She turned to one of the other men, a dark, gangly fellow with a stoop to his shoulders and a black wisp of a beard. Like Mara, he had folded himself into a chair. "Felicity?"

"Difficult to secure," said Sildar, his voice a rasp, his brows knitting over his aquiline nose. A varicose vein rippled in his smooth, brown forehead. "Just as I warned you it would be."

"It's not as if we have a choice," Laban told him. "The site was stipulated by the old man." Maybe *because* it was so difficult to secure—but that was an observation she had already shared with them. "I don't want to have to worry about Derek's muscle."

"I understand," said Sildar. "I'll do my best."

"Do your *very* best," she advised him, "or we may both have reason to regret it." She turned to the third man, a strikingly handsome fellow with chocolate-colored skin and light green eyes. "And you, Emphalelo? What can *you* tell me?"

The black man—who had chosen to remain standing—seemed to lose focus for a moment. Then, in a voice that sounded too deep and resonant for his modest frame, he said, "He is what he appears to be. There's no deception in him, no hidden agenda. But he is not naïve. He seems to understand the environment in which he will be immersed."

Emphalelo was a sensitive—an individual who could observe and then analyze a person without ever meeting him in person. His contributions had proven valuable in the past. Laban hoped they would be helpful in this instance as well.

"He *should* understand it," she replied. "He lived in it until just a few years ago."

"There were those who lived in it," Emphalelo rejoined, "who also managed to die in it. Familiarity does not always translate into understanding."

Laban had to concede the truth of the observation—but she chose not to do so out loud. These three were already too pleased with themselves.

"What's the best way to influence him?" she asked Emphalelo.

The black man thought for a moment. "Appeal to his sense of justice. That's why he is making the trip in the first place—to see to it that people like LeFleur are not mistreated in the wake of Mr. Ciejek's demise."

Laban might have come up with that answer herself. However, she felt more confident hearing it come from Emphalelo.

Before she could ask anything more of him, she heard a soft beeping. It alerted her that someone was attempting to communicate with her. She had an idea who it might be.

"Should we leave?" asked Mara.

"No," she said. "Stay."

Swiveling in her chair again, she turned her attention back to her computer screen. With a touch of a key, she sent Andar's image away. It was replaced by that of Owen Broadhurst, the lawyer.

Laban had worked with Broadhurst for some time now. In fact, he had been in Gregor's employ when she arrived. But even with Emphalelo's help, she never felt that she had gotten to the bottom of him.

On the surface, Broadhurst was frumpy and ill-kempt, a man so consumed by the law and all its myriad permutations that he had little concern with fitness or personal hygiene. He always seemed to be exerting himself even when he was just sitting there, a perpetual sheen of perspiration on his forehead. And yet, he wasn't overweight nor did he have any particular weakness for food.

To Laban's knowledge, the lawyer had but *one* weakness. Following his gaze to the vicinity of her partially exposed cleavage, she was pleased to see it hadn't gone away.

She didn't mind his looking. She was proud of her body, keeping it toned through careful diet and a strict exercise regimen. Like everything else she did, it was controlled and planned.

"Broadhurst," she said by way of a greeting.

The man looked up at her face and dabbed his forehead with a handkerchief. "Laban," he responded.

Their relationship had always been a cordial one in that they worked for the same man—first Gregor and then Karl. But they had never been what one might call allies. After all, she was concerned with profit and Broadhurst was concerned with legalities, and the two were on occasion mutually exclusive.

"How's the law?" she asked, priming the pump.

He chuckled humorlessly. "Increasingly complex, as you can imagine. National boundaries in northern Asia are only now beginning to resolve themselves. The colonies will feel the repercussions—economic and political—for years to come."

"Sounds like a lot of work."

"It is," he said. "The Interplanetary Court system is besieged with cases. It's worse than when the Christian Terrorists were tried."

Laban remembered, though she was still a little girl at the time. The courts found that religious institutions that taught hatred and approved of violence were liable for deaths caused in their name.

"Imagine if that ruling came down during the Crusades," Broadhurst remarked.

Laban smiled. "Might have saved everyone a lot of suffering."

"Would have changed the course of mankind, I would think," Broadhurst agreed.

"And Andar?" Laban asked, finally getting to the reason for the conversation. "How is he?"

"He's well," said the lawyer. But he refrained from elaborating.

Ever so slightly, Laban frowned. "Has he said anything to you? About his intentions, I mean?"

Broadhurst smiled a little. "Unfortunately, I can't discuss that. Client privilege and all that. But I think you know how Andar feels about the family business."

"Now it's *Andar's* business," Laban noted, letting the words hang in the air.

The lawyer tilted his head like a dog. "You sound certain that it'll be given to him."

"You don't think it will be?"

"I've no idea," said Broadhurst, dabbing at his forehead with the handkerchief. "Remember, Derek stayed when Andar left. The old man had to have taken that into account."

"Hard to imagine Derek in charge of the family," said Laban.

"Anything is possible," said Broadhurst, stealing another look at her cleavage. "In any case, I should be going. There's plenty to do before we arrive at Felicity."

"Of course," she said. "See you there." And she watched the lawyer's image disappear, to be replaced by Andar's.

"Pouty little bastard," said Mara from the background. He had expressed the sentiment before.

"Maybe," said Laban, leaning back in her chair. "But don't underestimate him."

"Whatever you say." He pulled a deck of cards out of his pocket and began manipulating it single-handedly, as he always did when he had something to say and thought better of it.

Laban had always been impressed by the things Mara could do with playing cards. His fingers were short and stubby, not at all the fingers of a card sharp. Yet he had a talent for manipulating the pasteboards like no one else.

He wasn't just an intelligence specialist either. He could take care of himself in a fight. Many were the men who had heard his cultured accent and mistaken it for a sign of weakness—and lived to regret it.

"Wonder what game *he* plays," said Mara, referring to Broadhurst. "Probably something gentle like pinochle."

"Still," Laban reminded him, "he's our friend until he's something else. Go easy on him."

Mara fanned the cards out on a side table. Standing them on edge, he tilted them one way and then the other. He seemed to be wondering which way they should fall.

"Andar won't want the family business," rasped Sildar. "But he may take it anyway."

Laban looked at him. "What do you mean?"

"To sell it," said the gangly man.

Laban had never considered him very good looking, but he seemed to have a way with the ladies. He liked to conceal weapons on his person and dare women to find them—after they'd had a few drinks, of course. He claimed it worked every time.

"It's not an easy business to sell."

"I know that," said Sildar. "But Andar may not."

Selling would be the ultimate rejection of what the family stood for. Was Andar capable of such a thing? Laban had to admit she didn't know—so she turned to Emphalelo.

"No," he said, as if he had divined her question. "Andar wouldn't sell his grandfather's business. He knows how much misery it would cause—not least of all to him."

"And those he loves," Mara added, still tipping his cards this way and that.

Suddenly, Sildar swatted at the air. "Damn bugs," he spat. "I thought we left them back at the compound."

"Apparently not," said Mara, intent on his cards. "I had to kill one last night in my cabin."

Sildar's brow furrowed as he searched for the offending insect. Without warning, he slapped the back of his neck—and then studied his palm. Holding it out, he showed the others the remains of something black and ugly. There was some blood mixed in with it, which meant it had already drunk its fill.

"Mosquito," said Sildar, making no effort to hide his disgust. "My neck's going to itch like a sonuvabitch."

Emphalelo shivered as he stared at the mosquito.

"What is it?" asked Laban.

The sensitive looked at her. "Nothing. Just a chill . . ."

TWO

The dinner was Karl Ciejek's idea.

After all, they were a family. Andar's grandfather hadn't wanted the reading of the will to be the only event marking his passing. He had wanted his brood to celebrate his death as they celebrated everything—with a feast.

Or so his instructions went.

In fact, few family members would be coming—only those with a stake in the substance of Karl's will. For the most part, that meant Andar and Derek and their entourages. Oh, there would be a few others, like Karl's half-brother William and the twin sons of Karl's cousin Dora, for whom Karl had always expressed an affection. But they were just bottom feeders as far as the will was concerned.

The big fish were Andar and Derek, and everyone knew it.

"I know you're not looking forward to this," said Owen Broadhurst, looking uncomfortable as he sat in the corner of Andar's cabin.

Andar frowned as he clipped on his black bow tie. "As you know, Derek and I never got along as kids."

Broadhurst wiped his forehead with his dirty handkerchief, which didn't at all go with his black tuxedo. "There's an understatement if I ever heard one."

Andar glanced at him. He hadn't thought the lawyer capable of that kind of comment. "You don't like Derek either, do you?"

Broadhurst took a while before answering. "Without going into a lot of detail, nothing in life was ever handed to me. Derek got *everything* handed to him."

And then some, Andar mused.

He didn't know why Karl Ciejek's sons were so different from each other. They were raised in the same household by the same father. But where Gregor was evenhanded with his son, Bela never seemed able to say no. Which was why Derek seemed to get bored easily, usually at someone's expense.

"You remember your tenth birthday?" asked Broadhurst.

They were all a blur. "Not exactly," said Andar.

"Derek took a liking to this one gift—a terrarium full of Bellarian fire ants. You know, the kind that change color when they've eaten?"

Andar remembered now. He had barely unwrapped the thing when Derek grabbed it from him and ran away. He had wanted to go after the little bastard but his grandfather had interceded, saying he would get Andar another terrarium—which he did a few days later.

"Funny that you remember that," he told Broadhurst.

"Not so funny," said the lawyer. "I was the one who got you the terrarium in the first place."

Andar smiled at him. "Really?"

"Really." The lawyer dabbed at his temple. "Unfortunately, we have to endure Derek's company for a little while."

And not just at dinner that evening. The next morning, they were all scheduled to take a tour of the jungle, followed by a picnic luncheon. The will would be read in the late afternoon.

In the meantime, Andar's passenger transport would linger in geocentric orbit. When Broadhurst gave the signal, he and Andar would be retrieved from the planet's surface.

Less than two days, Andar told himself. It would be over before he knew it. *Yeah, right.*

He turned to the mirror on the wall. He had never worn a tuxedo in his life—until now. He wished Katarina were there to see it. She would have had a good laugh.

Andar missed her.

To conceal how much, he turned away from the mirror—and Broadhurst. "Ever been to Felicity?" he asked, feeling he had to ask *something*.

"Can't say I've had the pleasure," the lawyer replied. "But I understand it's not the most pleasant world in the galaxy. The family has made a lot of money from it."

By riddling it with mines, Andar thought. But what he said was, "Come on. Let's get this over with."

"Whatever you say," Broadhurst responded, getting up from his chair and triggering the door latch. Then he shoved the door open with an effort and stepped out into the corridor. But once out there he hesitated, looking left and then right.

"Hangar bay is to the right, down two decks," Andar said gently.

Broadhurst snorted. "Right."

The shuttle was ready for them when they reached the bay. It dropped from the belly of the ship and plunged into a fluffy white layer of cloud. At least it was fluffy white on the top. When they pierced the bottom of it and Andar looked back through an observation port, the clouds looked like dirty, gray rags.

It took nearly twenty minutes for the shuttle to get near the surface. By that time, Andar had seen the marks his grandfather and others had made on Felicity. Entire mountain ranges were scarred and denuded. Big, dark conduits cut across valleys to bring ore to the processing plants, which dotted the land like ancient metal coins.

In some places, the forests were still lush and untouched. Andar wondered how long they would remain so. He was still wondering when a hundred-meter-square section of macadam rose up to meet his shuttle.

As it set down with nary so much as a shiver, Andar noticed a larger, better appointed shuttle at the other end of the landing field. Derek was already down there, it seemed, no doubt eager to start the eating and drinking part of the program.

As the shuttle door swung out and up, Andar got a whiff of the air. The tang of ore processing was unmistakable. Trying to ignore it, he got out and joined Broadhurst in front of the shuttle.

They were halfway between a network of processing plants and a cluster of cream-colored geodesic domes, each a different size. Andar had seen dome towns before. Unless this one was very different, each dome held either an office, a store, a bar, a lab, or a set of living quarters.

Broadhurst fished a handheld device out of his pocket. As he activated it, Andar saw a little screen light up with directions to the dinner.

"It's this way," said the lawyer, and began walking.

They wound their way among the domes for maybe twenty minutes before Broadhurst announced that they had reached their destination. To Andar, it looked like pretty much all the other domes. Part of him was disappointed. Knowing his grandfather, he had expected something lavish.

Putting the handheld device away inside his tuxedo jacket, Broadhurst led the way through a set of safety doors. Andar went after him. *Into the lion's den*, he mused.

As it turned out, the place was to his grandfather's taste after all. The wood that comprised the floor was rich and dark, polished to a fine sheen. Tables for twos and fours were scattered about, each one graced with a scarlet tablecloth and a generous cascade of local flowers.

But there was no one there.

A moment later, Andar realized why that might be. At the far end of the dome was a set of doors that led to a second, adjoining dome. Through them, he could make out the figures of some of the guests.

He exchanged glances with Broadhurst, who gestured for him to take the lead this time. Straightening his bow tie nervously, Andar crossed the room, pushed the doors inward, and went to meet his fate.

Having cleaned and oiled his weapons, Bet-Karh was placing them in their slots on the bulkhead when a shudder in the deck plates beneath his feet told him something had changed. Without hesitation, he left his quarters and headed for the ship's main control room.

It took him less than two minutes to make it to the heavily fortified central facility. As he had expected, the clan's two leaders were standing on the bridge, disagreeing insistently in the lurid light. A half dozen or so of Bet-Karh's fellow hunters stood below them and to either side of the bridge, their gatherings defined by clan—of course.

It had become an old and unwelcome sight.

Bet-Karh's clan, led by the venerated Dre-Nath, valued the Hunt above all else and took everything they needed from their prey. Their uneasy brethren, led by the grizzled Kirs-Giras, chose to rely heavily on the technology they developed rather than claimed.

Bet-Karh saw merit in both arguments, and didn't much care which philosophy the clan adopted. All he wanted was for the bickering to stop. At this rate, they would do what their enemies could not—put an end to both their bloodlines.

The enclosure gradually grew louder with the clicking of mandibles and the pounding of fists on bulkheads. Bet-Karh looked to the clan leaders to end the acrimony. Unfortunately, they were too wrapped up in their controversy to notice.

It was only luck that Bet-Karh happened to glance at the unmanned pilot's panel and see the square blue stud on it blinking wildly. He knew what it meant, too. One of the scout ships the clan had engaged had discovered a world worthy of a Hunt.

One, no doubt, on which an armed conflict was taking place. After all, it was beneath Bet-Karh's people to hunt inferior prey. Only the kind that had already proven itself as lethal predators were fit targets for the blades of the clan.

Data began to scroll down the pilot's screen, providing details on the world in question: its location in space, its size, its atmospheric makeup, and its climate. Its inhabitants were members of a species Bet-Karh's people had hunted before. It looked perfect.

But the control panel was turned away from the bridge, so the clan's leaders couldn't see it. If they didn't send a signal to the scout to put in a claim, the scout's crew would assume they weren't interested and alert another Hunter ship to the potential sporting ground.

Bet-Karh knew that if he interfered with the clan's leaders, he would be taking his life in his hands. But he couldn't let the opportunity slip away. Not when they so desperately needed a Hunt to heal the rifts in their clan.

Grabbing the thick metal bar that encircled the bridge, Bet-Karh vaulted over it and stood beside the two leaders. They whirled, ready to meet what appeared to be a challenge. But before they could deal with him, he stretched out his arm to indicate the pilot's panel.

All eyes slid toward the data screen. Suddenly, Bet-Karh's presumption was forgotten. The clan's leaders moved toward the pilot's console, reading the data and exchanging comments.

By the time they got there, they had made their decision—a joint one. In a gesture of magnanimity, Dre-Nath allowed Kirs-

Giras to press the blue stud, claiming the indicated planet on behalf of their clan.

Bet-Karh breathed a sigh of relief—not just for himself, but for everyone on the ship. Finally, they could look forward to a Hunt!

The last time Andar had seen his cousin, Derek was overweight and petulant, an overgrown adolescent. That was what he had expected to find in the next dome. But he couldn't have been more mistaken.

Derek Ciejek was as fit as anyone Andar had ever seen. His chest and arms strained under his tuxedo, pumped up like melons. His waist was trim, shorn of the fat that had always attended it. Even his face looked different, lean and chiseled where before it had been fleshy and amorphous.

"Cousin!" Derek exclaimed, blue eyes glittering beneath dark brows and a brush of equally dark hair.

"Derek," Andar replied, not knowing what else to say.

His cousin came forward and embraced him, careful not to spill the glass of dark red wine he held in his hand. Andar was so surprised, he found himself returning the embrace—if only a little.

Up close, he could see the brilliant blue dagger tattooed on the side of Derek's bull neck. Or rather, he could see part of it. The rest slid below the top of Derek's starched white collar.

"It has been too long," said Derek. "Welcome to Felicity. May her bounty be one in which we all share!"

As the words settled uneasily around Andar, a waiter swam past, conveying a tray of cold hors d'oeuvres. Derek plucked one, but didn't eat it right away. He was too intent on his cousin's response.

"Sounds good," said Andar, still at a loss.

Was this really Derek? They hadn't said a civil word to each other since they were tiny. The last thing Andar had expected was a warm reception.

"Nice to see you," said a feminine voice.

Andar turned and saw Celia Laban, his father's operations chief. She was wearing a shimmering, forest-green grown that hugged her taut curves and was slit up one leg. Derek smiled at her.

"If I can impose," Laban told him sweetly, "I'd like to have a moment alone with Andar."

Derek's smile widened. "Of course." And he moved off to join some of his men, whom Andar recognized. Especially Kaganas. He remembered *stories* about Kaganas.

Laban took Andar's arm and steered him toward one of the room's two bars. "Let's get you a drink."

He asked the bartender for a vodka with a lime twist.

"Lime's an expensive additive around here," Laban said. "Fortunately, the budget can handle it. Since I arrived here yesterday, I took the time to look around. This planet could be exploited a hell of a lot more than we're exploiting it now. Have you read the mineral content specs?"

"Can't say that I have," Andar responded, accepting his drink from the bartender. Actually he had read them pretty thoroughly, having little else to do on the transport ship.

"On the other hand," Laban said slyly, "maybe it's time we let this planet heal. What do you think?"

Andar had to chuckle despite himself. "I think you're trying to feel me out, maybe get an early reading on my intentions with regard to my inheritance—even before the will is read."

Laban feigned shock. "Whatever makes you say that?"

He was glad she had decided to make light of it rather than play shadow games. Laban had gone on Gregor's payroll after Andar left, but he had heard a few things about her. None of them did her justice.

Katarina, he thought, and urged himself to keep thinking it.

"Tell me," he said, "you're in the compound from time to time, right?"

She shrugged her bare shoulders. "Couldn't avoid it if I wanted to. Not if I'm to look out for your father's businesses."

"When did Derek get so . . ." He searched for the right word.

"Mature?" she asked. "When his father died. It was as if he finally grew up. But don't let the family feeling fool you. He's still a bastard of the first order."

"True," said Andar, eyeing his cousin, who was entertaining a circle of his hired help with some story. "But he's a more polished bastard, I'll give him that."

"Frankly," said Laban, "I'm hoping that's all you give him. But it's your fortune. You can do with it as you will."

Andar looked at her. "You're assuming I'll be left something after I walked out on the family."

"Yes," she said, "I am."

He wondered if she knew something he didn't, or was only guessing like the rest of them. Laban was sharp, or so he had heard. He wouldn't have put it past her to wheedle a forecast of the will out of someone.

Though if Broadhurst didn't have one, it was hard to imagine someone else did.

Suddenly, Andar felt a pair of hands on his shoulders. "Hey kid!" said a gravelly voice, and a familiar one.

Turning, Andar found himself looking into the scarred, grizzled, and obviously inebriated countenance of Pavel Trynda, one of his father's men for as long as Andar could remember. Trynda took him by the shoulders and squeezed, demonstrating the kind of strength Andar remembered from him.

"Look at you!" said Trynda, a curly gray lock of hair falling into his eyes. "The spitting image of your father!"

No one else had ever seemed to think so, but Andar didn't argue the point. "Good to see you too," he said, and meant it. Of all his father's muscle, Trynda had always been the most playfully childlike.

A sly look came over Trynda's face and he leaned in close. "Hey," he whispered, "you want this cooze?"

Andar gathered that he meant Laban.

"She sure as hell wants you," he said a bit too loudly. "When dinner's over, she'll be happy to tuck you in."

Andar glanced at Laban, who was smiling tolerantly. Obviously, this wasn't the first time she had seen Trynda in his cups. Andar was relieved. He didn't want to see the old man get fired.

"Actually," said Andar, "I'm in a relationship."

Trynda barked and made a gesture of dismissal. "Who isn't?"

"Excuse me," said Derek, rejoining them, "but I only agreed to give Miss Laban a *moment* with my cousin." He smiled at Broadhurst, who stood at the periphery of the conversation. "If you don't believe me, you can check the transcript. Right, Counselor?"

Broadhurst mumbled something beneath his breath. Derek couldn't have understood it any better than Andar did, but he went on anyway.

"Come on," he said. "There's someone I want you to meet."

"And what if he wants to stay right here?" Trynda demanded.

There was a moment of silence, into which all pretense of civility seemed to disappear. Then Derek clapped Trynda on the shoulder. "Be a good sport, all right? I haven't seen this guy in a thousand years."

"It's all right," said Andar.

With a sound of disgust, Trynda turned and went back to join the rest of Gregor's hired muscle. Derek looked pleased.

"We won't be long," he told Laban. "Then you can have him the rest of the evening, I promise."

Laban knew better than to pick a fight she might not win. "I'll be waiting," she said.

Andar allowed his cousin to direct him to the far corner of the room, where they joined a striking redhead in a blue dress.

"This is Marlene Noyes," said Derek.

"Pleased to meet you," she said, her voice soft but obviously intelligent.

Andar was impressed by the firmness of her grip. "Andar Ciejek," he said.

"I know." She laughed. "Doesn't everyone?"

"Marlene is my operations manager. Like Ms. Laban."

Andar was surprised. He would have thought Derek's ego too big to allow someone else to run the shop.

"You must be very talented," Andar noted.

When he left the family compound, he'd had no idea how big and complex the Ciejeks' business was. Now, with some experience under his belt, he did.

Noyes smiled. "You have no idea. If there's anything I can do to sharpen your focus on family matters, don't hesitate to ask."

Her gaze was frank, unflinching. Finally, it was Andar who had to turn away. Laban, at least, had been subtle about her overture. Noyes had all but grabbed him by the crotch.

Katarina . . .

Looking for a diversion, Andar found it in an argument flaring up by the nearest bar. Minh, one of Gregor's men, was getting in the face of Kaganas, who was nearly twice Minh's size.

With his muscular shoulders, his hairless skull, his long, square jaw and his oversized hands, Anton Kaganas looked like he was chiseled from rock. He went to work for Derek's side of the family shortly before Andar's departure. Rumor had it that he had killed more than a hundred men, none of them quickly.

Andar had always been told not to mess with Kaganas, even if he *was* Karl's grandson. The man's reflexes were simply too quick. Minh had to know that too, but he seemed not to care.

Andar's father had always liked Minh. Unfortunately, Gregor wasn't alive anymore to intervene on Minh's behalf. That left Andar to do it.

The good news was that it would take him away from Noyes, and temptation. With that in mind, he moved in the direction of the bar.

"You're out of your fucking mind," Minh said when Andar was close enough to hear him.

Kaganas shook his massive head. "If you don't have the right cask it's all rubbish. Look what happened when Macallan was forced to use casks from Africa rather than Spain. You couldn't drink that stuff!"

"New techniques are being developed," Minh insisted.

"You've bought into that propaganda bullshit," said Kaganas. "It *has* to be used casks, and it has to be aged a minimum of three years. Anything else is expensive piss."

"He's right," Andar said, unable to stop himself.

Both Minh and Kaganas turned to look at him. Eventually, so did all the hired muscle gathered around them.

"It's all in the maturation process," Andar explained. "You have to use used casks. The very best, Macallan, only used intact casks from a region of Spain. But, after the third ecological fuck-up, a lot was lost—including, it would seem, the ability to make a good scotch."

Derek looked at him askance. "How do you know all that?"

Katarina's family had been in the Scotch distilling business. But Andar didn't feel comfortable discussing that in this company.

"I just know," he said.

No one seemed to have anything else to say, all of a sudden. It seemed he had taken all the air out of the argument. But for Minh, that was probably a good thing.

"Anyway," Andar continued, "I'll stick to my vodka."

"Now that," Derek said, as he steered Andar back away from the bar, "is something you can make on any damned planet."

"True," Andar conceded. "But better on some than others. It can be exquisite or it can taste like shit. It depends."

By then, Noyes had gone her own way. Andar was happy about that. Derek was still there, of course, but in a funny way Andar was enjoying his cousin's company. It was such a novelty.

"So," said Derek, scanning the rest of the gathering, "how many of these guys do you still recognize?"

Andar named them. "On my dad's side, there's Minh, LeFleur, Trynda, Sildar . . . let me see . . . Zedolik, Dambrava, Abelkis, Mariano . . . I guess that's it. On your side, Kaganas, Wachman, Jurgens, Ibrahim . . . and that one with the patch, what's his name?"

"Turgeon."

"Yeah. Him. Funny that so many of them are still around."

"Good help and all that," said Derek. He sipped his wine. "If they do the job, why change? You look at Jurgens, a great motivator . . . you can't find guys like that anymore."

Andar took note of the man. Jurgens, whose hairline had receded almost to the middle of his skull, had been part of the Ciejek operation forever. According to Gregor, Jurgens was incredibly well read, a habit he had acquired waiting around for his services to be required. The one time Andar had talked to him, it was about Shakespeare.

Go figure, he thought.

"Unfortunately," said Derek, "age catches up with everyone. Look at us, we're the 'next generation.' Funny isn't it?"

"I suppose," said Andar, sensing that his cousin was leading up to something. As it turned out, he was right.

"So," said Derek, "what happens if you get your dad's piece of the pie?"

Andar glanced at him, unable to resist. "You afraid I'm going to take over?"

For a moment, the old Derek came through. Andar found himself enjoying it. Then his cousin regained control.

"No fucking way," Derek said congenially. "You ran out on the family, left it all for the rest of us. You may get your dad's piece in the will, but it still won't be yours. Not until you earn it."

There was no venom in his tone. He was speaking the truth, and they both knew it. But then, Andar had no intention of claiming anything. He had decided that even before he left Earth.

"Besides," said Derek, "let's be honest—what do you know about the business?"

"I know you step on people," said Andar.

A muscle twitched in Derek's temple, but he kept his cool. "I do what I have to. Just like your father. Just like our grandfather. You've seen this planet. Do you think I'm the one who did that?"

It was then that Andar noticed the silence around them, the air of expectation. All eyes were turned to him and Derek. Had they been talking that loud? Or had people been trying harder to hear them?

He hadn't intended to confront Derek. It had just happened. But it wouldn't go any further if he could help it.

After all, Derek was right about Karl and Gregor. They had raped planets and people. They had built their fortunes on people's suffering. He had said so himself, hadn't he? So why would he be upset hearing it from his cousin?

"I think," he said, "we ought to let this drop."

Derek looked at him for a long time. Then he laughed—a guttural, unpleasant tone that carried across the vast room. "You always were the good one, the nice one in the family. Grandpa Karl thought you were the best of us—until you made it clear you hated him and everything he built."

"I never hated him," said Andar.

"Of course not. You're too good for that."

Noyes had joined them while Derek was talking and put a hand on his arm, as if to calm him. "They're calling us in to dinner," she said.

Still glaring at Andar, Derek straightened the lapels of his jacket. "Yeah," he said, "let's eat. Try not to judge the food too harshly, cousin."

And he moved away in the direction of the adjoining dome.

"You didn't think it was going to be easy," said Broadhurst, "did you?" He was standing beside Andar, unnoticed until that moment.

Andar smiled. "I suppose not."

THREE

Sitting in his quarters, another glass of wine in his hand, Derek Ciejek chewed the inside of his mouth. Marlene and Jurgens, nursing drinks of their own, faced him from across the room.

"So?" he asked, prompting the two people he trusted most.

"I wouldn't underestimate him," said Jurgens. "Kid was always smart. And whether he wants to admit it or not, he's got some Ciejek in him."

"Yeah," Derek said, "I remember."

He recalled all the times he tried to push Andar around at family gatherings. It never ceased to amaze him that the younger boy had such spunk. It just made Derek want to push him even more.

"He's not interested in the business," Marlene observed, sinking down into her chair. "Not even if he gets a piece of it in the will."

"I got that, too," Derek said.

Despite the physical strength he had worked so hard to achieve, he prided himself more on his ability to read people. It was this attribute that had enabled him to consolidate and maintain power after his father died.

"However," Marlene added, "that doesn't mean he won't take whatever he might inherit and sell it—not just to assuage his conscience, but to stick it to *you*."

As always, Derek found himself drawn to her voice, smoky and alluring regardless of the time of day. He found her years earlier doing back-office work for one of his company's vendors, and he saw her ambition. She proved to be eager and compliant in bed—that wasn't a surprise. But afterward, she said some things he found interesting.

Ways to save money. Ways to increase his volume. Ways to keep his people happy. The kind of stuff he hadn't expected to hear in the sack.

He began giving her more to do. She mastered each task quickly and looked hungry for more. He promoted her and kept on promoting her, and before he knew it, his bedmate was his top lieutenant.

Funny how things had worked out.

"You really think he'd try and stick it to me?" Derek asked.

"In a heartbeat," Marlene said.

He glanced at Jurgens, who nodded in agreement.

"Then it's a good thing we've got that covered," said Derek.

He drained his glass and put it on the table in front of him, uncertain if he wanted a refill or if he was done for the night. Whatever buzz he had built up and maintained throughout dinner was wearing off. He was feeling tired and drained.

"You want to see Denholm now?" asked Jurgens.

"Absolutely," said Derek.

Jurgens put his drink down and left the room. Moments later, he returned with a ruddy, middle-aged man in gray coveralls, whose watery eyes peered out from behind a pair of thick glasses.

Derek figured the man was single, devoted to his technology, and fascinated by things larger than life. He was a loser, the kind the Ciejeks routinely used up and ignored by the handful.

"This is Malcolm Denholm, Mr. Ciejek," said Jurgens.

Derek nodded. "Talk to me, Denholm."

"Good evening," Denholm began, maintaining what he no doubt believed was a sense of dignity. He waited for a reply and received none. Swallowing, he began to talk, getting faster in the telling.

"I was able to tap into UNISC's databanks . . . that is the United Nations Interstellar Settlement Corps . . ."

"I know what they are," Derek said, wanting his guest to get to the point as quickly as possible.

"Yes, sir. So I tapped into their databanks and managed to copy certain communications among these aliens . . ."

"The Predators," Derek clarified.

"Yes, that's what we call them. No one knows what they call themselves. What we do know is that they work in clusters, families perhaps, or consortiums."

Ciejek waved a hand dismissively. "Whatever."

"Yes, sir." Denholm swallowed once and proceeded. "We know their frequencies so I took pre-recorded communiqués— the kind they would get from one of their scout ships—and turned them into a series of narrow-beam broadcasts, the idea being to get the attention of one of their larger vessels."

"Good thinking," Derek said. The comment brought an idiotic smile to the man's face. "But how did you know where to direct the signal?"

"By hacking into the UNISC network, I was able to intercept reports from an investigation team that just surveyed the remains of a colony on Harmony. I did some educated guessing and sent the communiqué in that direction."

Derek grunted. "So the word's out. Any response?"

Denholm pushed his glasses back onto the bridge of his nose. "My telemetry tells me that one of their ships is en route."

"Really," said Derek. "How far is it?"

"It will arrive tomorrow if they maintain their speed."

"Tomorrow," Ciejek said, and repeated it to himself softly.

He and his people had conceived this plan weeks earlier, when they saw that Karl Ciejek's health was failing. But it had been so theoretical. To his knowledge, no one had ever tried to summon the aliens before.

Now that it was happening, it was hard to believe. His mind whirled as variables were weighed, discarded, and reconstructed.

"All right," he said at last. "Andar's touring the forest in the morning. We've just got to direct the signal so the aliens will run into him."

Denholm looked perplexed for a moment. "Ms. Noyes already asked for that. It's been arranged."

Derek eyed Marlene and saw the cat that swallowed the canary. Damn, she was good.

"Excellent," he said. "That's the kind of news I like to hear. Well done, Denholm."

The technician beamed at the praise, unaware that Jurgens had approached him from behind, a length of something long and thin wrapped around each hand. Derek looked from Denholm to Jurgens and nodded just once.

The garrote quickly slipped in front of Denholm and tightened around his neck. The man flopped around like a marionette for a moment. But his struggles were in vain, given the ferocity of Jurgens's hold. It was all over in less than a minute. His body went limp.

"Nicely done," Derek said, getting up from his chair. "You'll find somewhere for the good Mr. Denholm to retire?"

"Sure thing, Mr. Ciejek," said Jurgens.

"I think I'll take a walk, then," Derek told him. He waited just long enough for Marlene to link her arm in his before leaving the room.

The air outside was cooler than he expected and he shivered once as he made the adjustment. Marlene must have been cold too, because she pressed closer to him.

"You're feeling pretty pleased," she noted.

"Why not?" he asked. "I just solved my business problem. What's not to like?"

"I always thought these Predator things were a legend, like the headless horseman," she said.

"Now you know," he replied. "And whatever you've heard about them, they're worse. Andar won't last ten minutes from the time they arrive."

"What about the rest of us?" she asked.

"I got it all figured out," Derek said, but he kept his plan to himself.

The aliens were stone cold killers. After they snuffed Andar—and whoever was with him at the time—it wouldn't matter what it said in his grandfather's will. Everything would go to Derek, nice and legal. And with Denholm out of the picture, there was nothing to tie him to the aliens.

And the best part was that he could sit back—with Marlene, if he chose—and watch the buggers in action. He glanced at her, knowing how much even a little violence excited her. What the aliens were going to do to his cousin would soak her panties but good.

He laughed at the image. It was a loud laugh, late at night and on an empty street between two domes, and it echoed.

Bet-Karh had avoided the bridge since he vaulted onto it unbidden, not wishing to remind either Dre-Nath or Kirs-Giras of the insolence with which he had interrupted their disagreement. However, he was eager to see the hunting ground for which they were headed. Fortunately, there was another facility on board from which he could see their destination close up.

Alone in the auxiliary control room, a backup facility installed by the species that had owned the vessel originally, Bet-Karh called up a schematic of the planet in question. Their scout ship had sent back data concerning size, strength of gravitational field, rotation, and revolution, as well as atmosphere, water, soil, and the like. Also, an analysis of the beings they would be hunting.

They were human. His kind had hunted them before with satisfying—and occasionally not so satisfying—results. He had heard stories of their cunning, their resourcefulness.

They also had a penchant for technological improvements. One moment they had ridden beasts across the land, the next they were in orbit and reaching for the stars. The important thing was that they would present his clan with a challenge.

This was an opportunity, a chance for his kinsmen, old and new, to hunt as one. To run their prey to ground. To take trophies worthy of their ancestors.

Bet-Karh could barely wait.

FOUR

Bet-Karh didn't understand.

He stood on the bridge of his clan's ship, shoulder to shoulder with the rest of his clan, and watched their leaders express their shock. Both Dre-Nath and Kirs-Giras pointed to the data screens in front of them, at a loss for an explanation.

The transmission from the scout ship had seemed so promising. But now that they were close enough to scan the planet themselves, with their ship's own sensors, they couldn't find any evidence of the conflict they anticipated.

No! Bet-Karh screamed inside, anguished by the prospect of being denied the Hunt.

How could the scout ship have made so grievous an error? Or was it they who had made the error? Had they followed the wrong course somehow, reached the wrong coordinates?

Dre-Nath, disgusted by this gut-wrenching turn of events, made a gesture of dismissal. It wasn't directed at anyone in particular. But Kirs-Giras, already on edge because of the disappointment he saw in his kinsmen, seemed to take it personally—and made a gesture of his own, without question an insult.

Another clan leader might have reacted violently, touching off a civil war within the confines of the ship. But Dre-Nath wasn't just any leader. Refusing to take the bait, he reached past Kirs-Giras and activated a diagnostic function on the pilot's control panel.

After a moment or two, a dull orange light came to life on the panel, indicating that the diagnostic was complete. But when the data screens refreshed themselves, nothing had changed. The world they described was all but barren of prey. Only in one small area was there any sentient life at all.

Once again, Dre-Nath manipulated the pilot's controls, bringing up more detailed information about the planet's population. The ship's computer identified them as humans. That part of the scout data, at least, could be confirmed.

Bet-Karh articulated the opinion that they still might have a worthy opponent on the planet's surface—just not a very numerous one. It wasn't a comment he considered before he spoke. It was merely an expression of hope.

One of the hunters from the other clan—a brash young pup—failed to take it that way. To him, it must have sounded like a taunt—a questioning of Kirs-Giras's ability to lead, perhaps. Bet-Karh couldn't get inside the hunter's head, so he couldn't know for certain.

However, the insult was clear. Deep beneath Bet-Karh's flesh, his kill-gland pumped, and he felt his body energized. Only his discipline training kept him from leaping on the pup and killing him. The hunter may have deserved to die, but it would be wrong for Bet-Karh to kill a member of his own clan—however extended it might be—especially in the presence of its two leaders.

But the pup wasn't done. He wouldn't be satisfied, it seemed, until he had provoked a combat. Bet-Karh breathed in, then breathed out. And still the pup persisted, his insults growing more and more barbed.

Out of the corner of his eye, Bet-Karh caught a glimpse of Dre-Nath. The leader's message was clear: *Do not respond.* Words were not worth a fight—not now, not when the clans needed to act as one.

Not only to engage in the Hunt, but to find out how they could have received such a signal from their scout ship.

Taking Dre-Nath's expression to heart, Bet-Karh looked away from the offending pup, ignoring him. He expected that he would thereby put an end to the altercation.

But his antagonist didn't seem content to let the matter drop. He stepped forward and challenged Bet-Karh to a single combat. Bet-Karh had exercised restraint to that point, but now events had gone too far.

He was about to draw his blade when Dre-Nath leaped from the bridge into the pit surrounding it. Inserting himself between Bet-Karh and the pup, he spoke quickly and fiercely. There would be no bloodshed, he insisted in no uncertain terms.

But in intervening unilaterally, Dre-Nath had taken a chance on offending Kirs-Giras. Hauling himself up over the rail, Dre-Nath rejoined his opposite number on the bridge. Their mandibles clicking rapidly, the two exchanged remarks.

Bet-Karh listened carefully, eager to hear the exchange. The more delicate the matter, the more artful the conversation. He recalled an old expression among his people: *Words, like weapons, should be chosen carefully and with full understanding of their use.*

Perhaps reason would win out, Bet-Karh reflected. He very much hoped so, for he was eager to go planetside and begin the Hunt. It had been quite some time since he ran free on an unfamiliar world, tasting its air, matching his skills against those of his prey.

The two leaders continued to talk for what seemed like a long time—and not just about Bet-Karh and the pup. Finally, their conversation ended and the two stood in silent communion before turning toward the data screens and studying the readouts once more.

When they spoke again, it was to every clan member in the enclosure. They made it clear to all that their decision had been made jointly, and that both sides of the clan must abide by it. The signal may have been a false one, they noted, perhaps even a deception intended to bring their ship to this world.

It had no native prey worthy of a Hunt, but it did offer a concentration of humans near the signal's origins, and humans had proven a challenge to other clans through the years. They would enter orbit and send down hunting parties. But they would not simply hunt. They would capture some of the humans in an effort to discover why the clan was lured there.

Only after they had obtained a satisfactory answer were the last of the humans to be turned into trophies.

FIVE

Derek Ciejek cursed beneath his breath and set his mug back on the table.

Casting a glance back over his shoulder, he asked, "Is this the best they can do?" But he already knew the answer.

The minerals present in Felicity's water supply made everything—including coffee—taste strangely tart. And no amount of filtering seemed to change that. Fortunately, they wouldn't be drinking Felicity's water much longer.

"It's the best," Marlene confirmed from the other end of the room, where she was packing the last of her belongings.

Rather than stay in one of the domes, they were in a rectangular box full of guest quarters not far from the mining colony's landing field. But then, Derek had wanted all his muscle around him, and none of the domes could have accommodated that.

Grumbling in response to Marlene's reply, he peered into the high-resolution, real-time display on the laptop computer in front of him, which showed him a clandestine line to the planet's operations center. His coffee sat to his left, right beside a half-eaten pastry of some unidentified nature.

"You're sure Andar won't catch on to us?" he asked Marlene.

"Mr. Denholm had assured me that the connection was secure and undetectable," she said, and not for the first time.

Derek nodded. "Just wanted to hear it again."

He looked back and forth between the keyboard in front of the display and the tiny screen of the handheld device beside it. Then, with a thick, manicured forefinger, he tapped one instruction at a time, glancing back and forth to make certain he was doing as Denholm—the *late* Denholm—had instructed.

After all, Andar had to be taken by surprise or Derek's plan would fail. That meant he had to do some fiddling with the planet's early warning grid.

He went about it slowly, meticulously, matching what was on the big screen to what was on the small screen and vice versa. *Take your time*, he insisted. This was the biggest gambit of his life and he was damned if he was going to screw it up out of haste.

Finally, he got the last set of instructions down. And to his satisfaction, it matched the small screen perfectly.

"There!" he spat triumphantly. Everything was as it should be. With a flourish, he used a forefinger to stab the execute key.

A moment later, he saw the confirmation message. Marlene must have seen it too, even from the other end of the room, because she yanked open the doors to his suite with both hands and called down the hall, "We're out of here in five minutes!"

Derek heard a series of responses from his men. The voices echoed, mixing with each other until they were unintelligible. The important thing was that they would be ready to go.

She closed the doors and returned to Derek's side. He chose that moment to finish the coffee, which somehow tasted better than before. But then, it promised to be a good morning.

The comm static he had created, thanks to Denholm's instructions, would resemble solar flare activity for eight hours—during which time Derek and his people would leave, and the aliens would arrive. They would be out for blood, too. He wished he could stick around to see it.

But then he would be as much at risk as Andar. *Not such a good idea*, he allowed.

"You think he'll suspect?" he asked Marlene as he got up from behind the computer and stretched.

"Andar, no," she said. "But Laban might."

"You think she's that good?"

"I know she's that good."

"You two should just get down to it already." Derek chuckled appreciatively as he tried to picture the women together. Shutting down his computer, he folded it up and tucked it into a padded black carryall.

"You'd like, that wouldn't you?" Marlene asked. "Unfortunately, there's not going to be much left of her, is there?"

Not after the aliens get through with her, Derek reflected.

"Come on," he said, allowing Marlene to carry her own luggage. He headed for the doorway, which would lead to the building's exit, which would lead to the macadam of the landing field.

"Let's get out of this shithouse," he said.

Normally, there would have been questions about the timing of Derek's impromptu departure, so close to the arrival of the aliens. But if all went according to plan, there would be no one left to pose those questions. Not a worker, not a waiter . . .

And certainly not an annoying younger cousin.

Andar felt the sweat trickle down his neck. Even though the sun wasn't terribly high yet in the bright blue inverted dome of the sky, the air was already warm.

His entire entourage, including his father's men, had joined him in his tour of the forest outside the mining compound. But then, they had little choice in the matter. His grandfather had insisted that they do so.

He had even picked out the man who would act as their guide, a fellow named Pablo Ortega who had lost part of an arm during a mining accident a couple of years earlier. Ortega was short, swarthy, and spoke too rapidly for Andar's taste, but at least he demonstrated a healthy respect for planetary ecology.

With a machete that was more for show than anything else, Ortega hacked away at the thick green foliage in front of them, leading them deeper into the forest. Andar was impressed by the variety of trees and plants he saw, all of which Ortega seemed to know by sight.

"I've never seen this much bio-diversity," Andar said.

Ortega stopped and took a breath. "It's your grandfather's doing. He worked very hard to keep certain species from going extinct."

"He did?" said Andar, surprised.

"Yes. I know it's easy to look around and see him as a rapist—someone who cared only about what he could pull out of the ground. But he decided long ago to restrict his mining activities to certain areas only. This was one of the areas he chose to leave inviolate."

"How do you know this?" Andar asked.

"Everyone on Felicity knows it. We saw the proof of it every day, in a dozen ways."

"My grandfather?"

"Your grandfather," Ortega confirmed.

"How many different species are here, anyway?" asked Laban.

Ortega smiled at her. "Our last inventory showed more than a hundred varieties of flora, thirty-five types of birds, fourteen kinds of arachnids, seventy-five insects, and three mammals."

"Why so few mammals?" she inquired.

"Despite Mr. Ciejek's efforts," said Ortega, "they were scared away by the mining. The noise, the changes in the salinity of the water table, and so on. It disturbed Mr. Ciejek that this was so. No doubt, he would have lured them back if he had lived long enough.

"Of course, this wasn't the only planet he owned. As I understand it, he tried hard to preserve parts of all of them, regardless of the manner in which his companies were exploiting them. So he perhaps can be excused if he didn't finish his work here on Felicity."

Ortega resumed his progress, pushing past a particularly thick and bushy branch and then holding it so the others could pass. Andar let Laban go first, then followed. Broadhurst, looking extremely uncomfortable in the heat, came after Andar.

"Mr. Ciejek always liked trees," Trynda noted, from further back in the line.

Andar glanced back over his shoulder. "Really?"

Trynda caught up to him. "You don't remember? Every day, he took a walk in the woods outside the compound. And if we were somewhere else, some other planet maybe, he would find a park or forest or jungle—somewhere to walk. What was it he said? 'To commune with nature.'"

Andar remembered the walks, now that Trynda mentioned them. When he was little, he went along on them. Afterward, as a teenager, he had believed himself too old for something so silly.

Images came to him of those late-afternoon hikes. Grandpa Karl led Andar and others—family members, even some of his men—for more than an hour sometimes. Unfortunately, some of those walks included Derek, who always grumbled incessantly.

Andar looked around at the trees, the alien blossoms, the birds sitting on the higher branches. He smelled the pungent scent of sap and heard the buzz of insect life.

His grandfather had chosen to love and protect this forest when he was living. It stood to reason that he would want to do so after his death. If Andar had a chance to help, he would do so—regardless of what was in the will.

Maybe he would even inherit this place. He liked the idea. Especially if his stewardship got in Derek's way.

Andar had always believed himself to be different from his grandfather. And yet, the old man had been a conservationist in his own way. Clearly, there was more to Karl Ciejek than his grandson would ever know.

Bet-Karh's clan leaders had questioned the ease with which their ship slipped into orbit around their target planet. After all, they had expected communications demanding that they identify themselves, followed by a military response. That was the way it usually went when they made their presence known.

But they had encountered none of that here. It was as if the inhabitants didn't care. Or even more bizarre, as if they welcomed the Hunters.

It was puzzling. However, a Hunt was a Hunt. They would find the answers to their questions soon enough.

Their strategy was to send down only one group of Hunters initially—just in case the humans had learned something from previous encounters and prepared some traps. Bet-Karh was honored as the consensus choice to lead the expedition. Then again, he would have made the same choice if he were leading the clan.

No one was stronger than he, or more skilled, or more devoted to the Hunt. It made sense to put him in charge. He would lead three others to the planet's surface—one from his original clan and two from Kirs-Giras's. Thus, two members of each clan would be present at the beginning of the Hunt. In everything, they had to observe a balance.

Now he was standing in a landing vehicle, dropping precipi-
tously through the planet's atmosphere, studying the scanner
data gathered by the clan. The planet was unremarkable, it
seemed, with the exception of the deep, gray scars visible in
several of the mountain ranges.

Humans had done such a thing on other worlds. It was the
way they obtained minerals for use in construction—that of
starships, for instance. Somehow, the sight rankled.

As a hunter, Bet-Karh preferred wide green jungles and lush
forests. However, one could not always choose one's hunting
ground. A hunter took what he could get.

Fortunately, the planet below offered plenty of green places,
plenty of spots where Bet-Karh and his people could remain
hidden. But only one of these places contained evidence of
humans.

They registered a bright green on the scans—nearly twenty
of them, moving in a single line through the densest part of
the forest. It was easy to tell them apart from the simpler life
forms, which registered blue or lavender.

Bet-Karh eyed the grid that the computer had automatically
superimposed over the screen. Pointing out the coordinates to
his pilot, he insisted they touch down nearby. But not *too* close,
lest they alert their prey to their presence.

The landing vehicle touched down some distance from the
humans, well out of range of their hearing. A check of the
atmosphere allowed the hunters to readjust their breathing
apparatus, mixing the chemicals they required to hunt at peak
efficiency.

The one thing they seemed to share with humans was
the level of gravitational pull at which they liked to operate.
Checking his weaponry one final time, a likely unnecessary
but at this point habitual act, Bet-Karh deemed himself ready
to engage in the Hunt. But in this instance, he was a leader.
Before indulging himself, he turned to assure himself that

the three with him were ready too. Helmets seemed to be in place, weapons at the ready; the ship had been secured and the security features would activate the moment their hatch resealed itself.

When they reached the surface, he led the way out of the craft and assessed their surroundings. Sunlight illuminated the ground. The sounds of wildlife surrounded them. Smells of all sorts abounded, mixing on the air. And there was no sign that their landing had been detected.

All was as it should be. The Hunt could begin.

With practiced ease, Bet-Karh led the small squad through the forest, paying careful attention to the sound of their footfalls. While he had honed the skills involved in tracking prey on the ship, most others in the clan had been less diligent. From the outset, he had been concerned that they would slip up. Instead, they earned his admiration as all four of them moved silently among the trees.

It took just a little while to find the first evidence of humans—discarded trash, easily discernible from the natural environment. Hunters, by contrast, never left waste lying about. It was an indication of disrespect for the hunting ground, and therefore for the Hunt itself.

Soon, additional signs became manifest, though these were more subtle: a footprint here, a broken branch there. Minutes later, Bet-Karh heard sounds—the grunting and squealing that humans used for speech. He raised a hand, instructing the hunting party to pause.

His senses alert, he tried to figure out how many humans might be nearby. The voices were varied enough that he could make out five or six of them, though there might have been even more. That was good—at least one target for each hunter.

Bet-Karh hoped that this would be the beginning of true unity between the two parts of his clan. The Hunt was said to heal a hunter's heart. With luck, it would heal the heart of his clan as well.

Lowering his hand, he used it to point out the way through the forest. Spreading out, the hunters advanced among the trees, each one eager to take the first trophy.

SIX

Ortega was in the middle of telling a story about his first encounter with a particular stinging insect when Andar heard a sound that didn't seem to match the others in the forest.

A *buzzing* sound. But not the kind an insect might make. It was too distant, too . . . mechanical.

While part of Andar dismissed it, another part focused on it. In all his experiences, both on Earth and other worlds, sounds that stuck out were always harbingers of trouble. The problem was that he couldn't identify it, and it was just one noise.

Could just be that my mind is racing, he reflected. *Could be I'm too distrustful of my cousin Derek.* Could be he was just plain wrong. After all, it was his first morning on the planet. What sounded out of place to him might be very much of a piece with everything else.

Still, you don't ignore your gut. His father taught him that long ago, and repeated it often enough that he couldn't dismiss it.

He tuned out Ortega's story and concentrated on the noises around him, searching for a repeat of the one that didn't sound right. But he couldn't detect any. He took a breath, let it out. He still wasn't satisfied, but it wouldn't do him any good to get himself twisted up about it.

However Ortega's story ended, it seemed to amuse Laban, whose laughter was surprisingly husky and uninhibited—not to mention sexy. The reaction seemed to please the tour guide, who gestured for the group to begin moving again.

When they reached the far end of the forest, they would break for lunch. After all, they were on a schedule. The reading of the will was slated for four o'clock in the afternoon, after which there would be another "family" dinner.

Andar was about to fall into line behind Ortega when he heard the sound again. This time, it was louder—closer. Laban had heard it as well, if the look on her face was any indication.

Then it wasn't just one sound, but a series of them, and Andar's fight-or-flight instincts kicked into overdrive. He looked around desperately for a hint of what was going on— and found one as a tree limb exploded beside his face, pulverized by a blast from a directed-energy weapon.

They were under attack. And he had no weapon of his own, no way to defend himself. For a moment, he hesitated.

Then he heard Laban yell, "Scatter!"

Before he knew it, she had broken to Andar's left, hurtling between two trees and almost immediately disappearing from view. Clenching his jaw, he followed.

Pavel Trynda was a loyal soldier. He had been with the Ciejek family his entire adult life. They were good to him and he had returned their kindness with unquestioning fealty.

He had a relatively cushy job at this point, he had stayed out of jail—unlike most of his family—and he had more than enough money to indulge his almost obsessive interest in pornography. While much of Earth's culture crumbled or was exported to other worlds, he amassed what he believed was an exquisite collection of videos and old printed matter. When visitors referred to it as erotica, he laughed in a guttural tone and always said, "Nah, it's straight porn."

And it was. Men with women, women with animals, women in bondage gear—name the variation and he had a sample of it. He had even come to study the history of porn, so he knew it was as old as mankind. He firmly believed that the first pictures men scrawled on cave walls were of naked women.

A moment earlier, he was imagining his next acquisition—a collection of nineteenth-century stereopticon slides found in someone's attic back on Earth, brought to his attention by a dealer. The next moment, he heard the word "scatter," and his mind changed gears.

Pulling out his laser pistol, he looked around for someone to burn. But he couldn't find anyone. That made him nervous. Trynda hadn't gotten this far without being a survivor. Though not necessarily accustomed to being in a forest, he understood the hiding places it offered.

Finding a thick, sturdy tree, he put on a burst of speed, cursed, and leaped—high enough to reach a likely branch. With an unaccustomed effort, he pulled himself up. He had never been known for his agility, even when he was younger, but his strength was enough to get him off the ground.

Grabbing a higher branch, he tested it once and then dragged himself up again. Though he didn't turn to look back—not yet—he tried to keep his ears peeled. But he didn't hear anything that would give away the location of his enemies.

Then he did—a sort of metallic buzzing sound. Certainly not something made by an animal. More like a giant insect, though he hadn't heard about any.

Had Derek set them up somehow? Trynda had no love for the little bastard. He might have worked for Andar, since he was Gregor's kid, but never for Derek.

Rather than stop to figure out the cause of the buzzing, he climbed higher, and didn't stop until he was a good thirty feet off the ground. The foliage was thicker at this level, blocking out much of the sunlight and masking noise. He couldn't hear the buzzing anymore—or for that matter, anything else.

All he heard was his own labored breathing. Damn, he was getting old. He had been in shape once. He had been a rock. But he had let himself get tired and soft.

Just as he thought that, he heard something after all—the crack of tiny branches on the forest floor. It sounded like someone big and heavy was walking around down there. But try as he might, he couldn't see the one responsible.

Of course, his vision was limited by the branches below him. It occurred to him that he might lower himself a few feet to get a better view. But now that he knew something was down there, he figured it was better to remain where he was.

That was why he didn't see the figure until it was staring up at him.

Trynda estimated it to be three meters tall and maybe three hundred pounds. It was covered head to toe in a strange, colorless armor that was only barely discernible against the native vegetation. It was also packing heat in the form of a projection from its shoulder, and maybe some other ordnance as well.

He fired at it, but he didn't have high hopes. His pistol wasn't made to pierce armor. As he had feared, the beam sizzled where it struck but didn't do a whole lot of damage.

Gotta move, Trynda thought.

He knew he was at a severe disadvantage. But he wasn't dead yet. Better to take his chances trying to escape than to offer himself up as an easy target. He looked around for the most promising route. Selecting one to his left, he reached out for the nearest branch—and spotted three red dots just above his wrist.

There was a brilliant white light and the sound of a small explosion. It took him a moment to realize that what had exploded was his arm.

The pain was indescribable—a burning unlike anything he had ever felt before. Blood pumped out of the stump in thick, red spurts and the remnants of his sleeve were aflame. But he didn't dare let go of his branch with his other hand, so he alternated between blowing at the flames and screaming.

Somehow, Trynda forced himself to look down at his attacker. The figure was still standing at the base of the tree, its neck craned so it could look up. For the first time, Trynda noted what appeared to be dreadlocks fanning across its broad back.

Trynda felt nauseated and his eyes began to lose their focus. He was going into shock. He knew he had to do something to survive but he couldn't imagine what it would be.

Should he let himself fall, hoping to come down on his assailant? No—the fall would likely finish Trynda as well.

The armored figure didn't seem to be in a hurry. He just stood there, gazing up at his adversary. Then, as if he had finally made up his mind, he raised his arm and took aim.

Trynda scrambled back on his branch, clinging to it with his good hand, until he was pressed against the tree trunk. He hoped that he had managed to hide himself from sight. But he saw the three red dots again, this time on his thigh.

Gibbering with dread, he slid forward on the branch again, trying to avoid a lock. A prayer came to his mind. He didn't know where it came from, but he muttered it anyway.

Finally, he was too weak from loss of blood to keep fighting. Dully, caught in the cold, hard grip of resignation, he watched the dots settle on his abdomen.

A second later, the white-hot plasma bolt struck home, cutting him in two and punching a hole through the trunk. The last thing he knew he was falling . . .

Run.

The word struck home again and again in Ortega's mind, plunging like a dagger into soft flesh, as he tried to keep pace with the woman Laban. He had no clue what had spooked her, but he heard the urgency in her voice and began moving his feet.

He knew little about the woman other than that she was Gregor Ciejek's operations chief, but the Ciejek name meant a lot to him. Karl Ciejek had been a criminal, yes, but he was also someone who cared deeply about Felicity.

No doubt, the men who had been behind him were criminals too, and likely armed. But Ortega was not. In fact, he had never fired a weapon in his life, not even for sport.

He didn't want anything bad to happen to the people entrusted to him, especially Karl Ciejek's kin. But even more desperately, Ortega didn't want anything to happen to *him*. He was just a miner, after all, one who had already given a piece of himself to the Ciejek family. He didn't want to give any more.

Suddenly, he felt something snare his foot and send him sprawling. He hit the ground hands first, so he wasn't hurt except for a few small scratches. But the fall caused him to lose sight of Laban, leaving him on his own.

As he got to his feet, he looked around—and saw someone come plunging through the foliage. It was one of the men he had led into the forest—the name escaped him. It occurred to Ortega to follow him, or at least get his attention; if he knew what was going on, it would be easier for him to avoid it.

But before he could say anything, he saw a flash of brilliance. Instantly, the man picked up speed and was driven forward into a tree—hard enough to snap his neck.

Ortega felt his heart start to bang against his ribs. He didn't want that to happen to him. He wanted to be back home, in the arms of his loving wife, in the safety of his everyday life.

But he doubted that whoever was attacking them would stop to ask who he was—a member of the family or a mere tour guide. *No, they will never do that.* So he hid himself, and quickly.

Swallowing down the heart that threatened to rise into his mouth, Ortega waited until he was sure there was no one coming to check on the man whose neck had snapped. Then he stood up a little and started off again. As he moved, he caught a glimpse of the dead man.

Something about his face was familiar. Or was it the awkward angle at which his head lay against the tree trunk?

Suddenly, Ortega knew where he had seen it before. The man he killed when he was a boy, the one who had taken his money in that poker game—he had looked the same way as he lay there in the morning light, strangled to death.

Ortega had never admitted to the crime, had never spoken about it, not even to his wife. Not even when the authorities accused someone else of the murder, convicted the fellow, and sent him to a penal colony. Not even then.

But Ortega had led a good life since that time. He had been a good friend, a good neighbor, a good husband. Surely he deserved to survive whatever was happening there in the woods.

Something sliced at his ear as he went by, and he stifled a curse. Touching a forefinger to the wound, he inspected it and saw a thin smear of blood. Some of the leaves around him were capable of inflicting even deeper cuts if he wasn't careful.

Speeding up again, he used his arms to push away hanging vines and low branches. Fortunately, he knew the terrain. He could tell that he was heading southwest toward an edge of the forest and the wide, open fields beyond.

It was in those fields that he would find the transport that brought them to the forest. If he could make it there unscathed, he would be home free. Maybe the others would find their way there as well. But whether they did or not, Ortega was going to use the transport to take off.

As he pelted through the forest, he came to a spot where the trees had grown closer together. They provided more cover for him, which was good. But they also slowed him down because it took longer to weave his way through them.

The longer Ortega ran, the more hope he was able to hold out that he was putting his enemies behind him. Finally, breathless from his unaccustomed exertions, he stopped for a moment and leaned against a tree, and looked back.

That's when he saw the impossible.

Not ten yards away, the air rippled. It was like a heat mirage, except it was close enough to reach out and touch. Then, as if some permeable barrier were being pierced, out stepped a figure from a nightmare. It was tall, broad, and armored, and it carried in its left hand what appeared to be a baton.

Ortega was so mesmerized, so afraid, that he couldn't move. It was as if he was rooted to the ground.

The figure's left hand twitched and the baton spun about, suddenly telescoping and more than doubling in size. It whirled around and around, gaining speed, becoming a blur.

Then, still in the hand of his enemy, it started moving in Ortega's direction.

The guide didn't dare turn his back on the figure, so he backed up. An unseen rock caught his heel and made him stumble, forcing him to steady himself by reaching for a branch.

The baton was maybe five feet away.

Ortega shuffled to his left, refusing to take his eyes off the spinning staff. This time he banged into a trunk, hard enough to shake himself up but not hard enough to inflict injury. He swung around behind the tree trunk, hoping it would shield him.

But he knew it wasn't thick enough. And now his enemy was only three feet away.

Ortega saw bits of metal catch what little sunlight came through the canopy above. He moaned deep in his throat. If that whirling metal hit him, it would slice him to ribbons.

Finally, the figure stopped advancing on him. But it drew the baton back, as if it was going to hurl it at Ortega. Desperate, he screamed out his willingness to surrender and fell to his knees, hands clasped together in silent prayer.

It saved him—for the staff whirred over his head and, with a *thunk*, splintered one of the trees behind him. The slivers of wood rained down on the forest floor.

It could have been him. The shock of that realization pulled him to his feet and started him running again. And his enemy didn't give chase.

Instead, Ortega saw as he looked back over his shoulder, the figure was moving toward its weapon instead. As he plunged through the woods, blindly this time, he knew he had one last chance to lose his pursuer.

Come on, he urged himself. *Run! Run for all you're worth!*

That was when the staff pierced his shoulder, an entire foot of its length emerging from the joint. Screaming in agony, Ortega felt himself pitch forward. And when he hit the ground, he stuck to it, because the protruding point of the staff buried itself in the forest floor.

The impact tore up his shoulder even more, sending spasms of red torment through his brain. And he couldn't do anything about it. Pinned to the planet itself, he was helpless.

Once more, the thing caught up to him, though it didn't seem to be in any hurry. *I love you*, Ortega told his wife, biting his lip against the pain. *I am sorry for the times I cheated on you, sorry for the man I killed, sorry for whatever else I may have done.*

It was then he heard the *klik* and turned his head, and saw the long, sharp blades that had emerged from the vicinity of his tormentor's wrist. The figure raised his arm and sliced downward, cutting deep into Ortega's flesh.

The pain was too much for him. He couldn't relieve it with his screams, couldn't dilute it the slightest bit. It was as if he were being consumed in fire.

Run! his mind urged.

His body, though, was long past being able to respond.

Laban had never before been so glad that she liked to keep in shape. She ran smoothly, fluidly, leaping obstacles like rocks and roots. But she couldn't seem to shake the sounds of pursuit behind her.

Finally allowing herself a glance back over her shoulder, she swore to herself. It wasn't an enemy dogging her steps. It was Andar.

That wasn't a reason to slow down, of course. She didn't know why they had been attacked or by whom, but she had to assume it was someone with perseverance—someone who would perhaps finish off the easiest targets first but would eventually come after all the others.

Laban had made a career of not being an easy target. She didn't intend to be one now either.

But it was getting warm in the loose togs she had worn to walk through the woods. *Too* warm. She could already feel the sweat collecting in the small of her back and under her arms. If this turned out to be an endurance test, she didn't want to overheat.

Stripping off her jacket, she flung it to one side. Too late, it occurred to her that it would give her pursuers a marker, an indication of which way she had gone. But what choice did she have? It was either ditch the jacket or ditch her chances of keeping up a decent pace.

After a while, she glanced over her shoulder again. Andar was still behind her, though his face was red and he was running a little ragged. Part of her hoped he would make it—though she wouldn't do a thing to help him if it affected her own chances of survival.

Suddenly, she heard a sound—a buzzing noise.

What the devil is that? she wondered.

She was still trying to figure it out when she heard another, more familiar sound—a human scream. It was long and loud and turned her blood to icy slush. Unconsciously, her hand dropped to her hip, where she carried both a gun and a knife in separate holsters.

Laban rarely went anywhere without protection, even a family hike. She was glad she had adhered to that policy.

As she thought that, she heard another cry. *Another victim,* she thought. Mara? Emphalelo? She hoped not.

Maybe Zedolik. The bastard had slacked off and needed to be fired anyway. But now wasn't the time for performance reviews.

A small leap carried her over a tree that had fallen long ago, most of it rotted hollow with age. An army of insects had turned it into their private domain and she was just as happy not to disturb it.

As she veered right to avoid a close-growing stand of trees, she heard something crack behind her. Permitting herself another backward glance, she looked for the source of the sound—and couldn't find any. She couldn't find Andar either.

Had he fallen prey to whoever attacked them? Or just fallen off the pace? If she lived long enough, she would find out.

Abruptly, the forest thinned out in front of her and she was bathed in sunlight. But did she want to be out in the open? *Only if I can find the shuttle,* she replied silently. But it was nowhere to be seen.

Slipping back inside the edge of the forest, she took out her gun and hunkered down behind a tree with her back to the open field. Then she waited. If anyone approached her from behind, she would have plenty of warning, plenty of time to react. And if anyone came out of the woods looking for her, she would be able to pick them off.

Unless there were a number of them.

But she wouldn't think about that now. She would just stay there and see what happened next.

Petras Zedolik knew two things. One was that he was alone. The other was that there was something bad out there in the forest.

His first inclination was to start running. For a moment, he did just that, planting one foot in front of the other, his heels pounding dead leaves to dust. Then he stopped and asked himself what the *hell* he was doing.

So someone fired at them. Big deal. He was armed too. If they wanted trouble, he would give them some.

Besides, the old man's grandson was somewhere not too far away, and he stood to inherit a chunk of the family's operations. He would be grateful to whoever kept him alive, right? *And it might as well be me*, Zedolik thought.

Trying to catch his breath, he looked around. He could hear sounds, but they were far away. And his eyes, which weren't as good as they used to be, couldn't find either friend or foe.

After nine years of working for the family, he had hoped the Ciejeks would reward him with something more than a weekly paycheck—a lieutenant's position, maybe. But Gregor had made it clear enough that Zedolik had reached the last rung in his ladder. He was a legman, a runner, a follower—but not a leader.

For a while, Zedolik had accepted this, figuring every team needed followers. If he served best that way, swell. But over time, he saw others gain favor and get better opportunities and he grew to resent the situation.

When Gregor died, and Karl went the same way, Zedolik figured he could start over. Sure, Laban had her opinions, and they weren't much different from those of the Ciejeks.

But there was the will. And Andar, who didn't know Zedolik or what he was capable of.

Zedolik's mother had always told him how important it was to make a good first impression. That was why he had acted like a gentleman at the family dinner, and why he had been so agreeable to going on the hike. It was also why he intended to find Andar and show him how valuable Petras Zedolik's services could be.

Yes, he thought, hearing a rustling in the trees overhead. All at once, a flight of big gray birds arrowed into the sky. He wished he could as easily join them. As he began to wonder what might have spooked them, he looked again at the branches above him.

The air there shimmered, and some squat, dark-colored thing appeared out of nowhere. Before Zedolik could even guess what it was, the thing moved, leaving the thick branch and dropping to the ground in a fluid motion.

Now, less than five feet away from it, Zedolik saw the thing was in actuality a humanoid. Heavily armored and laden with weapons, but definitely humanoid. Some kind of park ranger? A soldier on patrol? He rejected both ideas as idiotic.

More likely, it was one of their mystery attackers.

Raising his directed-energy weapon, he took aim. But before he could depress the trigger, the thing lowered its shoulder and drove him backwards into the forest.

The breath half-knocked out of him, Zedolik somehow managed to get his feet underneath him. *Shoot it!* he told himself.

But his adversary was quicker. He dealt Zedolik a back-handed blow that sent him rolling head over heels. Zedolik tasted blood and earth, and spat them out. Then he dragged himself to his feet and leveled his weapon at his enemy—who, inexplicably, didn't make another move to stop him.

Zedolik didn't ask why. He just depressed the trigger and stabbed the bastard with a blue-white stream of destructive force, and kept on doing so for several seconds.

Then he took his finger off the trigger.

To his amazement, his adversary was still standing. His armor was charred where the beam had struck, but otherwise he looked unmolested.

It was at that point that Zedolik realized he was a dead man.

He thought about running for it, but he knew that wouldn't accomplish anything. Strangely, he found himself getting angry. Angry at Gregor Ciejek for passing him over. Angry at Karl for insisting that they go to this god-forsaken world.

With a snarl, he reared back and threw his energy pistol at the armored figure with all his remaining strength.

The gun sailed through the air, tumbling end over end. But before it could strike anything, Zedolik's tormentor swatted it aside with its right hand. Then it drew back that same hand, which was festooned with sharp blades, and drove it forward again.

Instinctively, Zedolik raised both hands to catch the arm. But it was a futile gesture at best. His fingers, sliced to the bone by the alien's blades, failed to slow the assault down the least little bit. Numbly, Zedolik watched as the arm continued to shoot forward—straight into his chest.

He screamed, but all that emerged from his mouth was a pitiful whimper, and even that was cut short as blood began to geyser from his throat and pour out of his mouth.

His last thought was that Karl's grandson would have to fend for himself.

Andar cursed to himself as he watched Laban forge ahead of him and vanish into the forest.

She was obviously in better shape than he was—better shape than anyone, for that matter. One only had to look at her to know that. And she obviously had no intent of slowing down to let him catch up.

He didn't know who had attacked them. Derek was a possibility, considering the situation with the will and all the resentment he harbored. But the Ciejeks had more than their share of enemies, and any one of them might have decided to descend on them when the family was together in one place.

He heard the buzz again—the one whose source he couldn't identify. What in blazes was it? He was still wondering when he heard a scream—not the first he had heard in the last few minutes, but the closest.

He picked up his pace, though he knew he couldn't maintain it. And he didn't even know if it was getting him anywhere. For all he knew, he and his people were surrounded, and he was simply running from one adversary into another.

The last thing he expected as he drove his burning legs through the forest was to hear an old folk song in his head, something his mother liked to sing with him as a child.

He could hear her strong, lilting voice—a comfort to him, despite everything. The way the song was sung, it was supposed to accelerate with each chorus until it was nearly impossible to make out the words in the final stanza:

> *Now on that bird there was a feather,*
> *A rare feather, a rattlin' feather,*
> *And the feather on the bird,*
> *And the bird in the nest,*
> *And the nest on the twig,*
> *And the twig on the branch,*
> *And the branch on the tree,*
> *And the tree in the bog,*
> *And the bog down in the valley-o!*

It occurred to him that he didn't know what "rattlin'" meant. And thankfully, there were no bogs in sight, or it would be even harder to get anywhere. So really, the song was irrelevant to what was going on around him.

But it made it easier to run, somehow. And it took his mind off the buzzing, which might otherwise have driven him crazy.

> *Now on that feather there was a bug,*
> *A rare bug, a rattlin' bug,*
> *And the bug on the feather,*
> *And the feather on the bird,*
> *And the bird in the nest,*
> *And the nest on the twig,*
> *And the twig on the branch,*
> *And the—*

He stopped short when he caught sight of something in the distance. An armored figure, it looked to be about a head taller than most anyone Andar knew. And it had what looked like a directed-energy weapon mounted on one of its broad, powerful-looking shoulders.

He had never seen anything like it and was certain he never wanted to see anything like it again.

Fortunately, the figure had its back to him. It hadn't noticed him—at least, not that he could tell. But if he started running again, he would be giving up that advantage.

So, for the moment at least, he forced himself to stand still. It was easier said than done. His heart was hammering in his chest, his lungs pumping to get his body the air it needed.

Probably the best idea would be to back up—slowly, of course—and hope the figure didn't happen to glance his way. He was leaning in that direction when he saw the figure's head swivel.

Had he given himself away? *No*, he assured himself, *it's found something else. Something off to its right.*

Suddenly, the figure's shoulder-mounted weapon lit up and a burst of energy shot out. If it hit its target, Andar couldn't tell. But the noise the energy made as it sliced through the leaves gave him a perfect opportunity to become scarce.

Just like that, he was running again. But with each desperate breath, he expected to feel an energy beam skewer him between the shoulder blades.

SEVEN

High above Felicity, Derek Ciejek's ship hung in geosynchronous orbit, circling the world below it once every ninety minutes—give or take a handful of seconds.

Inside the vessel, sipping his coffee, Derek was comfortable and warm, freshly showered and smelling of talcum powder. He leaned back in the plush leather chair of his communications bay and regarded a series of monitors visible across the top of the main control panel. Under each screen was a digital display of data: location according to Felicity's master GPS satellite grid, ship time, and planet time.

He had tasked the ship's master computer to deploy a dozen video drones throughout the forest in a random pattern, hoping to capture the aliens' hunting methodology—because that might come in handy at some point—not to mention the grisly deaths of Gregor's men. As each drone found a person or alien, Derek was switching to manual control and directing the drone's motions.

As a result, he was recording a vast amount of information about the four aliens who had landed on Felicity. He was also finding the demise of Gregor's muscle great fun.

The only drawback to the drones was the buzzing sound they made. Derek found that the sound distracted both hunter and hunted. But it couldn't be helped—not if he was to have a bird's-eye view of the action.

"You don't find any of this disturbing?" Marlene asked, joining him in the bay.

Today she was all business, and her attire reflected it. The tailored outfit she wore had a stylish metallic thread winding its way through her navy blue and cream two-piece ensemble. She was the only one of his subordinates he allowed in the bay. The others were kept busy elsewhere on the ship so none of them would learn what he was up to.

In case things went wrong, the fewer who could drop a dime on him, the better. His father had taught him that, if precious little else.

"Ridding myself of the competition? Not at all." He watched an alien blast one of Gregor's men with the energy emitter mounted on its shoulder. "Man, I'd love to get my hands on that weapon. No doubt some science geek could tell me what it shoots, but it's damned effective. Get me a dozen of those and no one would ever bother us again."

"That's presuming none of your men burn their arms off," Marlene offered.

"Yeah," he conceded, "there's that all right. Some of these guys couldn't hit a target five feet in front of them."

"So, giving them even more deadly tools may not be your wisest course of action."

"Unless I upgrade the staff," he said.

Marlene laughed at the prospect.

But he was serious. Those weapons would change the balance of power in his dealings with other families. Andar wouldn't approve of such muscle, of course. But Andar wouldn't be around much longer to complain about it.

Marlene seemed to be attracted to one screen in particular, her fingers playing at the silver necklace that hung just below her collarbone. On the screen, an alien was moving from branch to branch, displaying more agility than seemed possible given the armor he wore.

"You can keep the guns," she said. "It's that armor that fascinates me. It doesn't seem to weigh them down, and it's remarkably flexible."

Derek considered the armor. He preferred weaponry and he always had, but there was something to be said for protection as well. After all, even mediocre help was hard to find.

"Okay," he said, "so get me a dozen of those too, and maybe my guys wouldn't burn their arms off."

He toggled to another drone, switching the perspective on the screen. There were only four screens available but nearly a dozen drones in motion, and he wanted to make certain he had one trained on his cousin. He didn't want to miss the confrontation between Predator and pain-in-the-ass.

The last time he saw Andar, he was trying to keep up with Laban. Where was he now? Was he having fun?

Derek found his cousin via Drone Nine. Andar was still running, still frantic to escape his attackers. *Go ahead and run*, Derek thought. The aliens would catch him eventually.

Derek nudged the controls, sending the drone in closer, but not so close that the noise tipped his cousin. He could see the red in Andar's cheeks, the rictus of effort on his face.

"Looks like he's on his last legs," Marlene observed.

Derek chuckled. "Serves him right."

It was a moment or two before he realized that Andar's flight was taking him into the vicinity of an alien—and the drone that was hovering not too far from it. More than likely, their paths were going to cross. If Derek played his cards right, he could see the confrontation from not one angle, but two.

This is going to be awesome, Derek thought.

He had no doubt that Andar was about to die. And with luck, he would capture it on both screens at once—not just for now, but for posterity. Whenever he felt depressed, he could play his recording of his cousin's death and cheer himself up.

The alien was moving slowly, deliberately, as yet unaware of Andar's presence. Its massive form crushed bushes, plants, and tree limbs without hesitation. The aliens were more powerful than Derek had imagined—even discounting their weapons.

Fascinated, Derek had the drone move in closer to the alien, hoping to get a really good look at the way its weapons related to its armor. He wondered if the stories about their ugly pusses under the helmets was true. This might be a chance to find out.

"What are you doing?" Marlene asked.

"What does it look like?" he shot back.

Closer, he thought, manipulating the drone's controls. *Just a little closer . . .*

Suddenly, the Predator's helmeted head turned in the direction of the drone. From Derek's point of view it seemed the armored figure was looking right at him—sending an unexpected chill up and down his spine, even though he was safe in his vessel.

"*Too* close," he said out loud, bemoaning his mistake.

"Apparently," said Marlene, without even a hint of irony in her voice. But then, she knew better than to mock him.

The last image before the screen went from Predator to static was of a brilliant burst of reddish light. *So much for Drone Eleven*, Derek thought.

On screen three, he saw that Andar had taken advantage of the distraction to get away at a run—saving himself, at least for the moment. But really, it was Derek who had saved him. He frowned at his cousin's good luck.

But Andar was still an idiot. *Don't get your hopes up*, Derek thought. *You can't escape them forever.*

Andar burst from the forest into a very bright and very hot open space. He hunkered down in the tall grass so as not to be seen too easily and tried to assess his location.

Isn't the transport around here? he wondered, using the back of his hand to wipe sweat from his forehead. If it was, he might be able to get away.

But he wouldn't. Not all by himself. There were still people back there in the woods who had worked for his father. He had come to Felicity because he felt a responsibility to them. Even with his life at stake, he couldn't just abandon them.

Of course, they might all be dead already. But he didn't know that for certain. He had to operate on the assumption that at least some of them were still alive.

One thing was for sure—he couldn't stay where he was. If his enemies were looking for him, they would find him out here quicker than in the forest. But where could he go?

He looked across the open fields at the mountains his grandfather had strip-mined before he was born. It looked like there was still some equipment on their slopes, some tracks and mountings for digging devices. Gaping holes as well, where miners had widened existing cave mouths or blasted access points.

How big were the holes? And how stable? At that moment, he would have given anything for a pair of digital binoculars. Without them, he could only hope that one of the holes might serve as a hiding place.

In Andar's front left breast pocket, his cellular vibrated. Ortega had warned them that communications in the forest would be garbled by the thick growth and spotty satellite coverage. Now, out in the open, his device was functional again. He unzipped his pocket and extracted the slim, golden device.

The message was from Laban. It read: *Out of forest. No sign of transport. You all right?*

Andar didn't know what she wanted, considering she had left him behind without a second thought. But she was one of his father's people. If he could help her, he would.

And if *she* could help *him* . . . well, that would be all right with him as well.

Since Laban was also clear of the forest, he called her. But he would keep it brief, in case the bastards hunting them were monitoring the radio spectrum.

"What do you see?" he asked as the connection was made.

"Mountains," she replied.

"Like they've been raped?" he asked.

"Yeah." Her voice sounded tired but not scared, which put her one up on him.

"The second lowest hole looks like our best bet," he said. He heard a slight tremor in his voice and didn't like it.

"Do you know who got hit?"

"No," he replied. "Anyone with you?" He had been keeping a tally in his mind—three screams, though there could have been many more.

"I've been in contact with Sildar. He's got Mara and Emphalelo with him."

"Tell them to meet us there, at the hole. And anyone else you can get a hold of."

Before landing, Mara had seen to it all their communications devices were networked and could be used to send out alerts in an emergency. The present situation certainly qualified.

"Any idea who the hell is after us?"

It was a reasonable question. "I think they're mercenaries," he said, "but not like any I've ever heard of."

"See you at the entrance," she said, and cut the signal.

Andar put his cellular away and assessed the distance between him and the mountains. It looked like a mile or so, though it could have been twice that distance. It was hard to say.

The height of the grass made it possible for him to hunker down and not be seen—at least not from the ground. But if he did that, he would lose speed. *Better to make better time and take my chances*, he decided, and struck out at the best speed he thought he could maintain.

He had made it about a third of the way to the mountains when he glimpsed someone else moving through the grass—about a hundred yards to his right and slightly ahead of him. At first, he thought it might be Laban. But the more he thought about it, the more he came to believe it was a masculine figure.

By then, the heat was starting to get to him. He could feel the sweat running down his neck and back. His legs ached, and he wished he had some water on him. However, he had dumped his canteen a few seconds after the attack came, not wanting it to slow him down.

Not that it had contained much water in the first place. After all, it was supposed to have been a nice walk through the forest, followed by a pleasant lunch. The drama wasn't supposed to have started until the reading of the will later that day.

Funny how things can change, he thought morosely.

He doubted that any of the other survivors, whoever they might be, had any water either. Or any clue as to what they were up against. Would their assailants ease off once they realized their targets weren't in the forest anymore? Or would they keep looking—and killing?

If they were going to do the latter, Andar was worse off than anyone. He knew nothing about directed-energy weapons. Hell, he had never even learned how to fight.

Neither his father nor his Grandpa Karl had ever trained him to do so. And he rarely got into fights as a kid, despite Derek's attempts to provoke him, so he had very little practical experience to draw on. He was going to need the help of his father's men, no question about it.

As the mountain drew closer, he spotted other figures—this time, to his left. Three of them, scattered across the open field. This time, Laban was one of them. Her silhouette was unmistakable.

If anyone in their party were to walk away from this, it would be her. *Maybe I ought to give her Katarina's contact information*, he thought sardonically. *Just in case.*

Even with his life at stake, he couldn't help looking at the terrain from an ecologist's point of view. The mountains, for instance, were tall and tightly clustered together, evidence of a major upheaval in the planet's earlier years. And the foliage at the top of the slopes, which was a significantly darker green than at the bottom, suggested that the soil changed with the altitude.

It was too bad the highlands contained the minerals his grandfather coveted. They looked like they had been rather beautiful until he carved the hell out of them.

Andar looked back over his shoulder. There was still no sign of the armored figures. That was a good thing—unless they were just intent on scouring the woods before they offered pursuit.

As he ran, the mountains seemed to recede before him. He was reminded of the myth of Tantalus, the poor soul in Greek mythology who was consigned to Hell for his crimes on Earth. Every time he reached for a bunch of grapes, which seemed to be well within his grasp, the grapes pulled away from him. That was how Andar felt about the mountains.

But eventually, he closed in on the base of the mountain that was his destination. When he got there, panting and soaked with perspiration, he found a narrow but well-worn path that seemed to lead to the tunnel mouth he had picked out. Someone was already using the path up ahead of him, though he couldn't tell who it was.

With another look over his shoulder to make sure the hunters weren't in sight, Andar turned and started climbing. He found himself looking forward to the shade he would find in the shadowy tunnel mouth, not to mention the prospect of being hidden from his enemies.

It took him some time to make his way up the three hundred feet to the level of the entrance. With a sigh of relief, he felt the darkness fall over him like a shroud, shielding him from the heat of the sun.

"You all right?" asked the man who had preceded him up the trail.

Andar squinted in the darkness, trying to make his eyes adjust. Finally, he recognized the fellow. It was Steponas Abelkis, a tall, thin, pale man with delicate, almost feminine features.

Abelkis had been hired by Gregor about the time Andar left the family compound, so Andar didn't know him very well. But he remembered his father being impressed with Abelkis, who always seemed to know how to move the most amount of material from point A to point B with the least amount of hassle. It was a handy talent in any business, but more so in the kinds of enterprises that required some illicit transport now and then.

"Fine," said Andar. "Thanks." Hearing the scrape of footsteps, he turned to watch the others approach.

Laban, Mara, and Emphalelo. But no Sildar.

Andar asked about him.

"He went back to see if he could help anyone else get out," Laban explained.

Andar's respect for the man immediately doubled. But having seen what they were up against, he didn't hold out much hope for Sildar's chances.

"Any idea who hit us?" Abelkis asked.

"None," said Laban.

Andar turned to Mara. "Could it have been my cousin?"

Mara shrugged. "He's capable of it, no question. But that muscle out there—I've never seen anything like it."

"Me either," said Emphalelo. "They were cold. So cold they didn't even seem human."

Andar felt a chill climb his spine. He wasn't a sensitive by any means, and he wouldn't have thought to express it that way, but he had gotten the same feeling. *Cold.*

There were sounds at the tunnel mouth. Everyone but Andar and Emphalelo pulled out their weapons. But the men who entered the tunnel were their comrades.

One was Sildar, looking mean and frustrated. The other two were Minh and Mariano.

"That's it?" asked Laban.

Sildar shook his head and jerked a thumb over his shoulder. Turning to follow the gesture, Andar saw Broadhurst make his way into the tunnel mouth. The lawyer was red-faced and disheveled, and he walked as if his legs weighed about a hundred pounds each.

"The rest," Sildar said definitively, "didn't answer. More than likely, they're dead."

Broadhurst planted his back against the wall and allowed himself to slide down to the stone floor. "My god . . ." he whimpered.

Andar swallowed. They had entered the forest with twenty-one people in their entourage. Eleven of them were unaccounted for, including Ortega the guide.

"Trynda's gone?" Minh asked incredulously.

Mariano blinked, looking stunned. "He owed me money."

"He owed *everyone* money," Mara noted.

"Then I get his collection," said Mariano. "I should be able to sell it for something."

"My god," Broadhurst exclaimed, his self-control obviously stretched to the breaking point, "we're being hunted by god-knows-what and you're thinking about pornography?"

Mariano shrugged.

"You may not be alive long enough to enjoy it," Laban snapped.

Mariano shot her a look, but remained silent. Obviously, he respected Laban, even in this situation.

"So what the hell are we supposed to do?" Minh asked. "Sit here and wait for them to find us?"

"It would help," said Sildar, "if we knew what they wanted."

Everyone exchanged glances, but no one was able to contribute anything on that subject. No one except Broadhurst, apparently.

"They're Predators," he said, his voice swollen with emotion.

Laban turned to him. "What's a Predator?"

The others started pelting him with questions, all at the same time. Finally, Laban held a hand up for silence. "Let the man speak," she said, mindful of the tunnel mouth, through which their tormentors could come at any time.

Into the quiet that ensued, Broadhurst injected what he knew. "People in my profession," he said, "we trade information. It's like a currency sometimes, even more valuable than money. I was trying to settle a case on Bellerophon, one corporation suing another over breach of contract, when I heard about them."

"The Predators," said Andar.

The lawyer wiped his forehead with a tattered sleeve, smearing the dirt that had collected during his flight through the forest, and said, "Yes. The Predators. EarthGov has been keeping them a secret until now, and for good reason. They're not human. They're another species altogether."

"Aliens . . . ?" said Mara disbelievingly.

Minh swore beneath his breath. "You're shitting me."

"I wish I were," said Broadhurst. "They're a race of hunters, and they have been using Earth as a hunting ground for centuries. Maybe millennia. No one is certain."

"What are they after?" asked Sildar.

Broadhurst looked up at him. "Sport, apparently. They get their kicks out of tracking us down and killing us, much as we used to get our kicks out of hunting game."

"Wait a minute," said Abelkis. "We're not game. We're *people*."

"Not to them," said Broadhurst. "We're walking trophies, no more and no less."

"And we've never heard of them?" asked Sildar.

"There are seldom any survivors to make a report," Broadhurst explained. "And like any smart hunter, the

Predators don't destroy the herd. They just pick at it here and there."

Abelkis shook his head. "So every planet we colonize might be a deathtrap . . . and no one ever warns us?"

"Earth is on its last legs," said Broadhurst, glancing at Andar, "and it will never recover. So we need to keep moving people out to livable planets. If word ever got out about the Predators, people would refuse to migrate. It's a matter of survival."

"So," said Laban, "we either stay on Earth and let the toxins finish us off or we get ourselves hunted and turned into human-skin rugs. Some alternative."

"Remember," said Broadhurst, "we were being hunted on Earth for a long time as well. Staying home wouldn't mean we would be protected."

"This is bullshit," said Mariano, his mouth twisting with anger. "If EarthGov knew about these aliens, why didn't they track them down and blast them out of existence?"

Broadhurst chuckled nervously. "I don't know. Maybe the Predators are too scattered. Maybe they're more powerful than we are."

"Maybe EarthGov has plans for them," Andar offered, knowing how bureaucratic minds worked.

"Maybe that as well," Broadhurst allowed ominously. "In any case, the Predators have survived. And they're here on Felicity."

"Just like that?" asked Mara. "I don't buy it."

"Derek's got to be behind this," said Mariano. "Maybe he hired the bastards to take us down."

Broadhurst shook his head. "They're not mercenaries. They don't kill for money. They're hunters, for godsakes."

It made sense to Andar. The armored figures moved like hunters, like beings used to tracking and killing prey. But if they were hunters, there would be no reasoning with them, no bargaining.

It was a chilling thought—even more chilling than what they had been through already. Because if Broadhurst was right, the hunt wasn't over. It had only just begun.

Looking around the tunnel mouth, he saw the others coming to the same conclusion. No one looked happy about it, least of all Broadhurst. It was clear he felt sick at having been the bearer of such bad news.

"I guess," said Minh, "that scotches the idea of going back to the forest to retrieve the bodies."

A curse exploded in Mariano's mouth. "So what are we going to do?" he demanded.

All eyes fell on Laban. *Yes*, Andar added silently, *what*?

EIGHT

When Bet-Karh and the other three members of his party reunited at the appointed time and place, all but one carried trophies of the Hunt.

Heith-Rek had already begun to weave a finger into a chain of other body parts that he had chosen to wear like a bandolier. Kaj-Nal had tied a skull to his belt by the long, thread-thin tendrils that grew from it. And Mor-Jut had a pair of pelvic bones hanging from a strap around the back of his neck.

Only Bet-Karh himself had not taken a trophy. Instead, he had hunted down and dispatched a mechanical device that was floating about the forest. He believed someone was using the device to watch the Hunt, and therefore saw to it that its functionality was disabled.

Of course, his comrades' trinkets were but samples of what they would bring back to the ship when the Hunt was over. They hadn't extracted a single spine from the corpses they had killed and mutilated. But there would be time for that. For now, there was still work to be done.

After all, they hadn't managed to capture any of the seven humans they had caught with their first sweep, finding them more fragile than they had imagined—so they hadn't gotten an answer to the question of why they were lured there. Nor could they return to their ship without it.

And now they had another question: who had dispatched the flying device that Bet-Karh had destroyed?

Bet-Karh consulted the long-range sensor system in his helmet and determined that there were ten humans still alive—though none of them were still in the forest. They were in a tunnel some distance away, across a wide, treeless field.

Plenty of prey for the four of them. And beyond them lay the colony itself, teeming with possibilities.

The divisions that created so much tension on their ship could be erased on this world. Bet-Karh and his comrades had proven that the two clans could work together seamlessly. Ever since their landing, the four of them had been of one mind, placing the Hunt ahead of any petty squabbles that may have arisen.

Just as it should be, Bet-Karh thought.

Now he had a report to deliver to Dre-Nath and Kirs-Giras. His leadership of this Hunt was a great honor, but it didn't relieve him of his responsibility to his superiors.

With this in mind, he activated the communications device embedded within his helmet. When the link came alive, Dre-Nath and Kirs-Giras were both audible on the other end. Bet-Karh had expected as much. He had also expected to hear the clan leaders squabbling, and was not disappointed in that regard.

In the briefest terms possible, he described the situation to them, including his sighting and destruction of the mechanical device. Then he asked them how he should proceed. Naturally, Dre-Nath's perspective was different from that of Kirs-Giras.

Dre-Nath said he preferred a Hunt to an outright slaughter. For that reason, he thought that Bet-Karh should continue the Hunt with his three comrades, and that the rest of the clan should remain aboard the ship—at least until they understood the circumstances under which they had arrived there.

Kirs-Giras, on the other hand, wanted to send down additional hunters and overwhelm the humans with sheer

numbers—not just the ten in the tunnel, but the rest of the
human settlement as well. His clan had always benefited from
the application of superior odds, he said, and he saw no reason
to change this approach.

Dre-Nath cited, from memory, some of the early history of
their people. He spoke of how the tradition of the Hunt began,
and how the prey they encountered on that ancient day was the
worthiest of adversaries.

The fight lasted weeks, as the clans took down victim after
victim, surviving the attack of blade, the attack of water, and
the attack of fire. Whatever their prey used to defend themselves was matched and repelled. The kills were sweet, the
victory memorable.

Flooding the planet with hunters, said Dre-Nath, did not do
honor to the spirit of that Hunt.

Kirs-Giras disagreed. He noted that times had changed,
and that their hunting methods had to change accordingly.
He pointed out that the firearms used by humans had gone
from single-fire rifles to rapid-fire machine-operated guns in
just a few centuries. Now, he said, the humans used projectile
weapons and directed-energy bursts. Soon, they would match
the hunters' plasma cannons, and the rules would have to
change again.

Bet-Karh listened to the arguments presented by both sides,
allowing both leaders to voice their thoughts as well as their
rebuttals. The argument extended for some time, going back
and forth, until finally there was a pause.

It was then that Bet-Karh interjected his opinion. As
expedition leader, it was his right to do so. Having heard the
arguments of both clan leaders and applied them to his experience on the world, he recommended against a massive Hunt
at this time.

Better to start with the ten humans still in the vicinity,
testing their mettle and seeing if it was any better than that

of the humans they had already eliminated. No doubt, the ten thought they were safe in their hiding place. Bet-Karh, of course, knew better.

A small hunting party, he said, would also be in a better position to investigate the circumstances under which they had been directed to this world. It could move quietly, all but unnoticed. Any larger operation would likely botch the job.

Only after they had obtained the information they required would it be advisable to expose the rest of the world to the Hunt—assuming it was deemed a challenge to the clan.

As Bet-Karh expected, Dre-Nath approved his plan. Kirs-Giras had other opinions and wasted no time in offering them. But Bet-Karh tuned him out, only pretending to listen to the long-winded rant.

Those with whom Bet-Karh hunted, the next generation of that clan, were worthy comrades. They had overheard Bet-Karh's recommendation and nodded their heads in silent agreement. Such unanimity gave him hope that a composite clan could work, that it might even be stronger than the sum of its disparate parts.

In the end, Bet-Karh and Dre-Nath prevailed. The four hunters already on the planet's surface would be given one day-night cycle to catch up to the ten fleeing humans and find out what they wished to know. Any more time would be an insult, an indictment of their competence.

Bet-Karh doubted that it would take him and his party a quarter of that time. After all, the humans had yet to prove themselves anything more than a passing diversion.

NINE

"We need help," Andar said to the assemblage before him.

Everyone turned away from Laban and looked at him. For a moment, no one spoke. Then Mariano broke the silence.

"No shit," he said.

Laban walked over to the man and punched him in the gut. He folded, then stood up with an angry look. But he wouldn't curse her out. Not Laban.

She shot a glance at Andar. "Did you have something in mind?"

"There have to be a hundred people back there at the settlement. And we've got cellulars. They can come out with another couple of transports and get us out of here."

"They can," said Mara. "But if Derek was behind this, do you think he'll let them send out a transport?"

"And even if he's *not* behind it," Sildar added, "it'll take them a good half hour to get here, even at top speed."

"We can hold out that long," Minh judged.

Laban frowned as she weighed the proposition. "Maybe."

"For whom?" asked Mara. "A rescue party—or the Predators? If we use a cellular, they can trace the signal."

"What do you suggest?" asked Laban.

"We stay here," said Mara, "until dark. Then we skirt the forest and make our way back on foot."

"That's a forty-mile trek," said Abelkis. "Without food or water."

Mara shrugged. "You want to live?"

The tunnel got quiet. Mara's suggestion was the least risky, it seemed to Andar. But there was another option—one that no one had mentioned, but which had to be on everyone's mind.

"I can't help thinking," he said, "that these hunters are after *me* and not the rest of you. If we split up—"

"Forget it," said Laban. "We're in this together."

"But," said Andar, "if I—"

"But nothing," said LeFleur, who hadn't spoken a word to that point. "I worked for your father, remember? No way I'm letting you do something stupid."

The others weren't as vocal, but they seemed to share the sentiment. Andar sighed. He had never realized how much Gregor's people loved working for his father.

"Guess what?" asked Emphalelo, gazing at his open cellular. "We can forget calling for help. I'm not getting a signal anymore."

Andar opened up his own unit and saw he wasn't getting a signal either. Minutes earlier, they had transmitted text without any problem. For some reason, that was no longer possible.

"Either they've done something to the switching station," said Sildar, "or they've found a way to interfere with the signal. Either way, we're on our own."

Minh turned to Laban. "So we do as Mara says—and wait?"

She frowned. "Only until it gets dark. Then we move, and move fast."

Andar felt someone tap him on the shoulder. It was Sildar.

"What is it?" he asked the security chief.

Sildar reached inside his vest, withdrew an energy pistol, and handed it over to Andar. It was lightweight, made of a cobalt-blue brushed metal, with simple sight and trigger. Despite its minimal heft, it looked like it would pack a punch.

"An extra," said Sildar.

Andar studied the weapon for a moment, then tucked it under his belt. The metal felt strange pressing against his stomach—and not in a good way. But under the circumstances, he would get over it.

Toggling a drone control, Derek watched in fascination as his cousin turned the pistol over in his hands. He had to laugh at how little firepower Andar's men carried—except, of course, for Sildar, who was always armed to the teeth.

He wished the drones had audio capabilities but he would settle for an old-fashioned silent film—which only lost precious little definition to distance and the need to depend on infrared in seeing into the tunnel mouth. It was written plainly on Andar's face that his entourage had been outgunned and outmaneuvered. There was little chance they would find help before the Predators turned them into dinner, or whatever it was they did with their kills.

After seeing Andar take out his cellular a few moments earlier, he had asked his ship's engineer to set up an interference field in the vicinity. There would be no calling for reinforcements, no talking to one another if Andar's men split up again. In fact, no communication at all.

Derek could sit back now and enjoy the well-worn, comfortable leather of the communications chair, and the human drama unfolding before his hungry eyes.

He just wished he had thought to stock popcorn.

"Holy Mary," Abelkis cried from his watchman's position near the tunnel mouth. "They're coming!"

Everyone picked himself up and pulled out his energy weapon. Andar moved to join Abelkis, though he was careful to stay in the shadows. Laban moved with him, her features hard and unperturbed by the news.

Sure enough, there were four figures, all of them in identical armor, wading through the grass between Andar and the forest. They moved slowly, without any particular sense of urgency, headed unerringly for the tunnel where the humans were holed up. Obviously, they had figured out where Andar's people went.

"I get the idea they have ascertained our general location," said Broadhurst, dabbing at his forehead.

"We're going into the tunnel," said Laban, backing away from the entrance though she kept her eyes trained on their enemy.

But they had no notion of how deep the tunnel ran or where it ultimately led. To other tunnels, maybe? Was it a dead end— or did it let out somewhere on the other side?

This may be worse than being in the forest, Andar thought. And yet, what choice did they have? Only to meet the Predators head-on, and that wasn't really a choice at all.

"This time we stay together," Laban added. "Use your cellulars for light. It won't be much, but we won't *need* much."

Nods greeted the advice and everyone took out their units, now little better than flashlights, and held them at the ready. Their faces looked ghostly in the faint blue illumination.

Laban turned to Mariano and said, "You take the rear."

Mariano nodded and said, "Done."

Then they followed Laban into the gloom of the tunnel, moving at a jog. Andar fell into the middle of the pack, next to Broadhurst. He wondered if the lawyer, who didn't look like he was in shape, would be able to keep up the pace.

As they got deeper into the mountain, the tunnel got cooler. Before long, it felt downright cold. And the dampness of their clothes only exacerbated the situation.

The floor beneath them was worn smooth from the passage of men and machines over years and even decades. The walls, on the other hand, were rough-hewn. The lack of railroad-style tracks indicated that this was one of the smaller tunnels, and that the ore would have been pulled out from another one, a level above or a level below.

Bits of debris—plastic wrappers, discarded batteries, a half-torn photograph of a dog—could all be seen as they navigated the tunnel. Signs directed injured men to the medical bay a level below, and a digital display that should have shown how many days it had been since there was an accident was dark, its power cell drained to zero a long time ago.

Andar had done some spelunking with Katarina, but he had never grown fond of it. Not that he was claustrophobic. He could tolerate cramped spaces—he just couldn't understand the appeal of seeking them out.

For some reason, Broadhurst's cell seemed to cast more light than any of the others. Andar asked him about it.

"Truth to tell," said the lawyer, "I had it custom-made for that purpose. I leave every morning before my wife wakes up, so I need my cell to find my clothes."

It was small talk, but it cut the tension a little. And it wasn't endangering them because the scrape of their feet on the stone floor was a lot louder than their brief exchange.

Andar allowed his light to play along the ceiling and walls in the hopes of finding an offshoot from the tunnel—maybe a narrow one that the Predators, with their size, couldn't negotiate. He was hoping for a miracle. But all he found were outcroppings and piles of rock chips.

The longer they walked, the longer Andar had to wonder if the Predators had followed them into the tunnel. *Maybe their species likes enclosed spaces even less than I do*, he speculated. *Maybe hunting in a tunnel is too easy—like shooting fish in a barrel.*

Half an hour later, they were still descending deeper into the mountain and they hadn't received a single sign that the Predators were pursuing them. Finally, Laban raised her hand to signal a stop. Andar wondered why—until he saw the way the tunnel split up ahead. One tine of the fork angled down to the lower level, while the other went up.

Andar wondered if Laban would split up the group, to increase the chances that at least part of it would survive. She didn't, opting instead for strength of numbers. Starting along the "up" side of the split, she beckoned for the others to follow.

It was a steep angle, and they were tired already—Broadhurst in particular. But he wasn't the only one who had allowed his body to fall into a state of neglect. Mariano and LeFleur were panting hard, and Minh wasn't far behind them.

It was even cooler here, but by then Andar didn't feel the temperature anymore. He was too busy keeping up, and making sure Broadhurst did the same. A couple of times the lawyer had breathed his thanks for the attention, but they both knew it was only possible on a limited basis.

A few minutes after they had begun their ascent, Andar spotted a shape up ahead. He wasn't the only one, either. Laban and one of the others pointed to it as they approached it.

The shape stuck out from the wall, but it wasn't another of the outcroppings. It looked manmade. Laban paused to examine it in the light of her cellular.

The shape reflected the light, proving itself to be metallic. On closer inspection, Andar saw it was some sort of power-routing system. A moment later, Mara said as much.

"If we can tap into it," said Abelkis, "we may be able to light the tunnel for ourselves."

"And the aliens as well," Emphalelo reminded him.

"But for them, that might not be an advantage," Laban noted. "For all we know, the Predator species hunts better in the dark."

"At worst," said Andar, "we'll both benefit, and it'll be a wash."

Hunkering down in front of the system, he tried to find an indication of how much power was left—if any. After a few moments, he found a digital readout. Fiddling around with it, he got it to light up, indicating the system was still drawing power from the colony's energy plants.

He couldn't even begin to guess how long it had been since the system was used. Would it work? They would soon find out.

A moment later, he found what appeared to be the "on" button. Pressing it, he heard a whining sound.

He wondered which came first in the universe—sound or light. A flicker of illumination was the first sign of the latter. It became a dazzling strobe effect, which was followed by a series of lights coming to life further up the tunnel. Set into the stone of the ceiling, each one cast a pool of pale yellow on the floor below it.

It was good.

Seeing it, everyone put away his or her cellular and studied the path ahead. Not much further up, three more tunnels split off from this one—some with tracks, some not. Better yet, at least one track had a cart on it. If that had been left behind, maybe other things had been left as well.

Things we can use. Variables they could throw into the mix, if necessary—and Andar had a feeling necessary was coming pretty soon.

Laban looked like she had come to the same conclusion. But for now they had to keep moving, keep putting distance between them and their pursuers.

"Let's go," she said, and started forward again.

The light allowed Andar to see the walls around him a little better. The mining there had been done with exquisite efficiency. The excavations were tightly spaced together, letting little go to waste. Dark black streaks were seen in the gouges dug out of the rock walls; he supposed they might represent iron deposits.

He could also see now how each step kicked up some of the dust on the floor. Like everyone else in his party, he was covered up to his knees in a fine, brownish powder. And they were leaving footprints, which the Predators would find easy to follow.

As if on cue, a sizzling sound reached Andar's ears, followed by an explosion of dirt and rock. No one cried out but everyone surged forward into a run.

Everyone but Mariano, who stayed behind to give them cover.

Andar paused, thinking for a moment that he might stay behind as well. But he felt Laban grab a fistful of his shirt and pull him forward.

Because I'm not a good enough shot to be of much help? he wondered. Or because he was potentially her boss, if they got out of this alive?

Following her lead, he raced down one of the tunnels up ahead, hoping it wouldn't turn out to be a dead end.

Feng Kuan Minh heard a sound behind him like the ignition of a gas stove. Then he felt the ensuing explosion, close enough to burn his back.

Part of him realized that the Predators had caught up with them. Another part was grateful that Mariano had positioned himself between the hunters and the humans, because Mariano was a vicious sonuvabitch.

Bolting ahead, Minh couldn't tell which way the others were going. Forced to make a choice among tunnels, he chose one that had a set of tracks in it, and only the dimmest of lighting. It was only after he had entered the tunnel that he realized he was all alone.

It was long and the lighting was sporadic, pooling maybe every twenty feet. The shape of the walls was more uneven than in the other tunnels, but he couldn't find a niche in which to hide himself. The only option was to keep going.

Or it would have been if the Predators had come after him. But the more he listened, the more it seemed to him there was no one behind him. It made sense, didn't it? The bastards weren't necessarily going to run down every tunnel they came to—only the ones full of prey.

And there was just one specimen in this one. Hardly worth the effort, Minh hoped.

He had only seen the Predators from a distance, which made it impossible to accurately gauge their size. But in his mind's eye, they were big, broad-shouldered, and vicious. So big, in fact, that they could eat their victims raw.

But if they hadn't followed him, what did it matter how big they were? Or how vicious?

Minh's throat was raw already with the air he was forcing in and out of his lungs. His legs felt like lead. He wasn't used to this kind of exertion.

Since there didn't seem to be anyone behind him, maybe he could rest a while. *Recharge my batteries.* It didn't seem like such a bad idea.

He was still considering it when he came to the end of the tunnel.

A dead end, he thought, his heart sinking in his chest. *A goddamned dead end.*

But he still had a chance. If none of the Predators had followed him, he could double back as far as the last split—at which point he could take another tunnel or retrace his steps to the tunnel mouth. That was the last thing the aliens would suspect.

Yeah, he thought, *that's the ticket.*

Then he heard the footfalls from further down the tunnel. They were steady, measured, without the least hint of uncertainty. As he watched, his throat closing with fear, he saw a figure take shape in the distance.

It seemed to fill the tunnel from side to side. And the closer it got, the bigger it seemed in its leathery looking armor. Pieces of human beings hung from a string around its neck—hands, feet, and things Minh couldn't even identify.

As it came closer, he realized one of the pieces was a head. A head he *knew*. His gorge rising, he recognized it as Mariano's.

Cursing beneath his breath, he felt his eyes well up with tears. *The bastards. The mother-loving bastards . . .*

Raising his energy pistol, he fired, but the tears ruined his aim. And before he could fire again, the alien fired a blast into the lighting panels above them, plunging them into darkness and sending glass tinkling to the stone floor.

Still, Minh fired. Right down what he thought was the middle of the tunnel, though it might not have been the middle at all. It was impossible to tell now.

But he could hear the Predator's advance. It was getting closer to him. Closer . . .

His teeth grinding together, Minh transferred his pistol to his left hand and pulled out his knife with his right—twisting his hand around so the blade would be positioned for a back-handed slash, if it came to that.

As the Predator approached, he expected it to say something, to make a sound at least. But it was silent. He couldn't accept that, couldn't deal with it, so he did the talking himself.

"Going to blast me with your shoulder-thing?" he asked. "What are you waiting for?"

But his tormentor didn't give any indication it was going to fire. Nothing lit up or anything. It just kept coming, making a *slikt* sound like two knives scraping together. Minh didn't like it in the least.

Swallowing hard, he fired again. This time, his blasts seemed to connect with something—and ricochet about the tunnel, momentarily throwing the alien into sharp relief.

The sonuvabitch was almost on top of Minh, less than a dozen feet away. And as far as the human could tell, his beam hadn't done any damage to the alien's armor.

Minh wanted to run, to get away, to melt into the dead-end wall behind him. If he couldn't pierce the Predator's armor with his energy burst, what was a knife going to do? He whimpered a little, deep in his throat.

"Fine," he said, searching for bravado, "we can go toe-to-toe. You and me, pus-face."

"Toe . . . to . . . toe," came the reply from somewhere in the darkness.

It wasn't just Minh's words. It was his voice, and it sent chills down his spine. He didn't think the aliens even spoke English, and here was this one somehow throwing the human's words back at him.

"Toe . . . to . . . toe," the Predator repeated again.

Something snapped inside Minh. Lunging blindly, he struck with his knife, hoping to slip it between two plates of the alien's armor. He could feel the shock all along his arm as his weapon hit something hard and bounced off.

Suddenly, he saw a tiny red light in the vicinity of the Predator's shoulder. It projected a beam onto Minh's chest. *Go ahead*, he thought, *kill me.*

But there was no ensuing burst of energy. The creature just stood there, daring Minh to try again.

With his target in sight this time, the human blasted away with his energy pistol—to no avail. The alien's armor deflected each barrage. As a last resort, Minh went at his enemy with his knife again, but the blade slipped off the armor's surface and sent him lurching into the Predator's arms.

The monster grabbed the human's knife arm and pulled Minh to him. Then, with his other arm, the Predator placed Minh in a crushing embrace.

Up close, the creature stank. The stench made Minh want to gag, but he couldn't draw in enough breath to do so. Struggling, he tried to slip the alien's grasp.

When that failed, he stamped on the Predator's booted foot. The impact produced no response. Then Minh was lifted off his feet, until he found himself looking into the deep, shadowy eye lenses of the alien's helmet. Tiny eyes scrutinized him, seeming to pierce him to his very soul.

But just for a moment. Then he was thrust against the ceiling of the tunnel, the impact cracking ribs on both sides of his spine. Before he could scream, he was jammed into the ground.

This time, his skull fractured. He could tell even before he saw the blood dripping into his cloudy, unfocused eyes. But the Predator wasn't done with him. Kneeling beside him, it grabbed him by his windpipe and squeezed.

Black spots flooded Minh's vision and he heard the rasp of his final breaths. He tried to raise his hand—which somehow still had his knife in it—to stave off his tormentor, but he could barely move it.

The creature had such disdain for him that it allowed him to keep the weapon while his breath ran out. Minh's final, jumbled thoughts were a chaos of pain and despair.

Had he been alive to witness it, he would have seen the Predator reach down and take the knife from his lifeless hand, then use it to slice through Minh's clothing, and finally to skin the flesh from his human bones.

"And he would have heard these words as the alien worked: "Toe to toe . . . toe to toe . . ."

In the confusion of the Predators' arrival at the tunnel junction, Abelkis saw Minh duck into a tunnel on his own.

But Abelkis knew better than to follow Minh anywhere. The man had never had any luck at making choices in life. If he had picked that particular tunnel, then there had to be something wrong with it.

Instead, Abelkis selected a tunnel that had a set of tracks with a cart on it. But no sooner was he inside it than he skidded on some loose pebbles and lost his footing. Instinctively, he put out his hands to break his fall, and skinned them on the tunnel floor.

He smeared the blood on his pants leg and hoped the Predators didn't have a keen sense of smell. Otherwise the fresh blood would make him an easy target.

Crouching on the far side of the cart, he peered into the dimly lit tunnel. It went quite a distance before it dwindled from sight. Hence, the track and the cart, he supposed.

The cart itself was a durable steel construct but it had clearly seen better days. Dents marred all four of its sides and one of the interior handholds was missing. It looked big enough to hold four, maybe five miners, though all it held at that point was loose dirt and several good-sized stones.

The controls were intact, as far as he could tell. He considered jumping in and taking a ride so as to put more distance between him and the Predators. There was a risk, though—he had no clue where the track led and how structurally safe it was further down the tunnel.

Abelkis took note of a manual handbrake release and decided he would chance it. Carefully, he reached down and gripped the brake, wondering if it would make noise. Just then, he heard a scream, and what sounded like a rain of heavy footfalls.

They were getting closer to him. *It's now or never*, he thought.

Squeezing the brake release, he felt the brake unlock with a tiny click, probably too small to be heard amid the other noise. At the same time, the cart was drawn by gravity down the angled incline of the tunnel—slowly at first, but only because Abelkis was still hanging onto it.

Clambering inside it, he braced himself for a trip down the track at breakneck speed. As he feared, the cart made noise but it wasn't too bad and before he knew it, the entrance was receding. But he hadn't gone very far before the cart screeched to an unexpected and unsettling halt.

Gathering himself, he poked his head out of the cart—and saw a pile of rock on the track. At some point, it seemed, it had fallen from the ceiling of the tunnel.

He cursed to himself. If he wanted to keep moving, he had to clear away the rubble. And that might take some time—time he didn't have, if the sound of footfalls from further up the tunnel was any indication.

Maybe I can just push the cart through the pile, he thought. He tried. But it wouldn't budge. The wheels just wouldn't turn with so much debris on the track.

It was about that time that he saw something leaning against the rough-hewn rock wall to his right. It proved to be an old fashioned pick-axe. Since time immemorial, the tool of miners—simple, basic, and deadly.

Their energy pistols hadn't put a dent in the Predators' armor. But maybe an axe . . .

Abelkis was still considering the idea when he realized the footfalls were suddenly a lot louder. Looking down the tunnel, he saw a dark, hulking form that could only have been one of the aliens.

Sliding behind the cart, he took cover from the Predator's shoulder-mounted weapon. The alien might end up killing Abelkis, but at least he wouldn't be barbecued from a distance. He would have a shot against the monster at close quarters.

He didn't even take out his pistol. He just held onto the axe with both hands, caressing it like a lover—feeling the wooden handle, worn smooth from long use, and the tiny nicks in the metal blade. The axe had cut through who knew how many tons of rock over the years.

Maybe it could cut a Predator as well.

Abelkis knew there would be no time for finesse. Just a brief opening and a swing of the axe, and a hope that it would be enough.

Or at least that it would hobble the Predator enough for the human to get away. He would settle for that. In a heartbeat, he would.

His shoulder pressed against the cart, he couldn't see how close the Predator was. But he could hear the scrape of the bastard's bootsoles against the stone.

Slkkt. Slkkt. Like a knife scraping against a rib on its way to someone's innards. *Slkkt . . .*

Abelkis's mouth had gone dry. He could barely swallow. But his senses remained alert. It sounded like the Predator was just on the other side of the cart.

Not yet, he thought. *Stay cool . . .*

He heard the sound of something dripping, wet splotches hitting the tunnel floor and being absorbed. It was a sound that filled his mind with unspeakable horrors.

Not yet . . .

And then it was time.

With a roar of defiance, Abelkis leapt up from his crouch, raising the axe above his head. The Predator took a step back in apparent surprise, but didn't raise its hands to defend itself—either because it was too slow, or because it didn't feel the need.

With every bit of strength he had, Abelkis brought the axe down. He had aimed for the alien's shoulder where it met its neck, but the blade hit the Predator in the thigh instead—and managed to wedge itself deep in the armor there.

Suddenly, the tunnel was filled with an unearthly sound, like the chittering of bats. He had never heard anything like it before, but there was no question that it was a cry of pain. He had done some damage.

But he couldn't remove the axe. It was stuck in the armor, leaving him without the option of taking a second swing at the alien. The Predator continued to chitter wildly, its head thrown back—but at the same time, it grabbed the axe handle with both hands and began to pull.

Abelkis knew there was nothing to be gained by hanging around. Turning, he ran down the tunnel as fast as he could.

He managed to make it a few yards before he heard the axe fall to the ground. *Run!* he urged himself, though his legs were already burning with his effort. *Run!*

It was then that he saw the red light piercing the darkness ahead of him. It was coming from over his shoulder—and he knew why. It was part of the alien's targeting system. He had seen one of the Predators use it on another of Gregor's men.

As long as he could see it, he was safe. But a moment later, it vanished—and he knew that it had found his back. Cringing, he cried out in fear.

And was enveloped in a blue-white flame.

As he fell to the ground, every fiber in him screaming in unbearable agony, he realized that he was dying. But even as he perished, he got some small measure of satisfaction from the fact that he had given the Predator a taste of its own medicine.

In his ship, orbiting high above Felicity, Derek Ciejek switched from screen to screen, attempting to locate his cousin. The eleven remaining drones had been sent in and around the mountain, seeking any member of Andar's party—or better yet, the Predators. They were such superb trackers, he knew they would lead him to Andar and the others.

Then he remembered—the aliens had some kind of cloaking technology. If they were in clandestine mode, the drones wouldn't pick them up. Also, of course, it was possible that not all of the Predators had entered the mountain.

"Maybe they're being cautious," Marlene suggested.

She had joined him just minutes earlier, carrying two plates of food. He wasn't sure when he had last eaten, but once he smelled the grilled onions he knew it had been a while. Now the two of them sat there filling their bellies, watching the drone-fed screens as if they were at a gambling emporium.

Except Derek had already won, and he took pleasure in the certainty of it.

Unfortunately, reception wasn't as good as it could be, given the fact that some of the drones were deep inside the mountain. A little more light would have helped, but that would have drawn attention to them and potentially spoiled the spectacle.

Marlene pointed to one of the screens—the one in the upper right hand corner. "Is that one of Andar's friends?" she asked.

Derek followed her gesture. "Could be." He moved the drone in for a closer look and was greeted with the sight of a skinned corpse. The organs and bones seemed to be intact, but the flesh was gone and all the corpse's blood had pooled around it.

"Oh my *god*, that's gross," Marlene sputtered.

He grunted gleefully at her girlish reaction. "Yeah," he said, "but without its face, I can't figure out which mook that is." And identifying the bodies was half the fun of it.

These Predators were amazing. Just amazing. At this rate there wouldn't be a single member of Andar's party left by sundown.

He chuckled. "Looks like cousin Andar is going to miss the reading of the will, poor baby."

As Andar plunged through the tunnel before him, he had the worst feeling that one of the Predators was right behind him. But in fact, he saw when he glanced over his shoulder, the only one behind him was Owen Broadhurst.

The lawyer was red faced with his exertions, gasping as if he hadn't breathed in a day and a half. But somehow, arms and legs flying, he was managing to keep up with Andar.

Not for long, though, Andar thought.

Broadhurst's heart would give out before long. Or he would twist an ankle. Or something else that would keep him from going on.

Andar didn't owe the lawyer anything—not really. The guy was a hired hand, having made the trip to Felicity because he was being paid to do so. But he was one of Gregor's people, every bit as much as the others. Andar didn't want to see anything happen to him if he could help it.

So he slowed down a little and let Broadhurst catch up.

Unfortunately, they were both at a huge disadvantage. Though Andar was armed, he didn't have much experience with energy pistols. And Broadhurst probably had even less.

What's more, they had no idea what was going on behind them. They had heard some screams, but they didn't know who was dead and who was still alive, or where the survivors might be.

Or, for that matter, how to get out of this damned mine.

Andar tried to dredge up whatever he could about mining, hoping something would inspire a course of action. He knew, for instance, that every tunnel actually needed two paths, one for people and one for air. Depending upon the size of the air passage, they might be able to squeeze through it to the surface.

That is, he thought, *if we can find it.*

He also knew that mining tunnels tended to run into one another as the digging progressed, so it could actually be like a maze deeper into the mountain—which meant the Predators would have a tougher time locating them.

Or not. It depended on the tools the aliens used for tracking.

Suddenly, he heard a scream. It was faint, which meant it was far away. But it still twisted in his gut that he had lost another of his father's men.

Just a few moments later, he heard another scream—even fainter than the one before it. But it didn't sound like something formed by a human throat. It was more of an insect sound—something a giant cricket might have made.

Or . . . an alien? Was it possible that one of the others had taken down a Predator? Less than likely, but one could dream.

"Mr. Ciejek," Broadhurst rasped.

Andar turned to him. "Yeah?"

The lawyer pointed up ahead. "What's *that*?"

Andar didn't see what Broadhurst was talking about at first. Then he caught sight of a large, shadowy shape. It wasn't a Predator—too big for that.

As they got closer, he saw that it was a vehicle—one basically cylindrical in shape and covered in dirt. He wiped away some of it with his fingertips, revealing silver plating with a series of black numbers on it.

At first, Andar thought it ran on the tracks that bisected the tunnel. Then he realized that it straddled them, independent of them. He had never seen anything like it, but he was hardly an expert on the subject.

More importantly, the vehicle looked long enough and deep enough to fit half a dozen miners. *If I can get it open, and if it's still in running shape . . .* Getting inside proved to be easier than he thought—just a matter of clearing the dirt away from a touch-sensitive plate.

Inside, he saw a coil of heavy rope and six seats. Also, a control panel that looked too simple not to understand. Slipping into the driver's seat, Andar pushed what looked like the ignition—and felt the thing hum to life as if it had been overhauled just the day before.

Broadhurst looked at him, wide-eyed. "This is a miracle," he said.

It was. They had what they needed to escape the tunnels.

The lawyer slipped into the seat on the far side of the vehicle. "What are we waiting for?"

Andar frowned. He couldn't do it. "There may be survivors back there. I can't leave them."

The lawyer looked like he was about to argue the point, then stopped himself. "Whatever you say," he responded, looking uncharacteristically calm as he resigned himself to the situation. "But you know this is going to get us killed."

And in the most painful way. "I know," said Andar. But he still had to do it.

Unfortunately, it was too tight in the tunnel to turn the vehicle around. They had to back it up. How far depended on what they saw—and heard.

"We give ourselves five minutes," said Andar, "to gather whoever we can. Then we're leaving."

With that, he put the vehicle's transmission in reverse and started backing down the length of the tunnel.

Andre LeFleur had found two heavy, fist-sized rocks—filled, he imagined, with iron ore. Like an idiot, he had dropped his weapon in his haste to get away from the Predators, so he had to improvise.

With the rocks in hand, he traced his way back along the tunnel down which he had fled when the Predators appeared. His instincts told him to go the other way, to try to find an exit at the end of the passage. He wasn't going to listen to his instincts.

LeFleur had never been considered very bright. His main value to Gregor Ciejek had always been his brute strength. In fact, that was his value to everyone in his life—the fact that he was bigger and stronger than anyone else.

But that was enough to get him a job as Gregor's personal bodyguard, and then as Laban's bodyguard after Gregor's death. That was why he had accompanied her to Felicity. And that was why he was fighting for his life in a dark and deadly place.

LeFleur had heard the screams. He knew others had been tracked down and killed, and that it might soon be his turn to die. But he couldn't keep running—not as long as Laban might be alive and in need of his services.

As he lumbered along the tunnel, he heard a new sound—not a shriek of pain, but a scrape as of boot sole against rock. And he couldn't see who made it because of a bend in the tunnel.

If it was a Predator, he would never get past it to help his employer. His only option was to hide and hope the thing didn't spot him as it went by. Seeking concealment, he found a slot in the tunnel wall and squeezed himself into it, still grasping the rocks.

LeFleur could hear the scraping sounds get closer. But underneath them, there was another noise—a buzzing. At first, he thought it might have been in his ears, a result of the pressure down there under the mountain. Then he decided it was from somewhere else.

But he couldn't think about that. He had to concentrate on the approaching footsteps. The muscles fluttering in his jaw, he gripped the rocks in his fists a little tighter.

The scraping noise was coming closer. Closer still.

LeFleur felt his teeth grind together. He didn't dare to move, didn't even dare to breathe. But if the Predator spied him, he would have to be quick with his rocks. It was a difficult spot.

Then he heard a whisper: "Anyone there?"

It wasn't a Predator. It was a *human*.

Or was it some kind of trick? Might a Predator be forcing one of LeFleur's comrades to lure him out of hiding?

No, he told himself. *That would mean they suspect someone's in here. And if they suspect that, it would be easy enough to find me on their own.*

Fighting a feeling that he would regret this, he poked his head out—and saw the bedraggled form of Broadhurst, the lawyer. Broadhurst started at LeFleur's appearance, holding his hands up to protect himself. Then he saw who it was and heaved a sigh of relief.

"Andar has a plan," he breathed. "Follow me."

LeFleur didn't know what kind of plan it might be, but he liked the sound of it. He wasn't known for his speed, but he was quick enough to keep up with Broadhurst as the lawyer made his way along the tunnel.

"How much further?" LeFleur whispered.

Broadhurst turned to provide him with an answer—and instead, let out a shriek. Too late, LeFleur understood the reason for it, as something long and hard pushed its way through his back and came out just beneath his rib cage.

Writing in agony, LeFleur felt his mouth fill with blood. As it dripped down his chin, his knees buckled, no longer able to hold his weight. But he didn't fall. There was something holding him up, something immensely powerful.

Suddenly, he felt the thing inside him wrench sideways, ripping internal organs and causing him to moan in agony. He could feel his strength leaving him, his vision dimming.

But he could still see Broadhurst. He was staring at LeFleur, transfixed, his skin pale and his hands trembling.

From deep inside, LeFleur dredged up a command: "Run . . . !"

It came out as little more than a rasp, unintelligible. Then he remembered the rocks he had clutched in his hands. They were still there, despite everything.

Raising one of them, he threw it at Broadhurst. It hit the man in the shoulder, eliciting a cry of pain. No, *two* cries—one from Broadhurst and one from LeFleur himself. But it also woke the lawyer up, and little by little sent him scampering down the tunnel.

It was then that LeFleur was pitched to the ground. But he never reached it. The shaft inside him prevented that, propping him up several inches from the tunnel floor.

As the blood dripped from his nose and mouth, he saw a pair of boots appear in front of him. Had he been able to look up, he was sure he would have seen the armored form of a Predator.

Placing one of its boots on his shoulder, it plucked the metal shaft out of LeFleur's back. The wave of agony that followed was indescribable. A scream tore from LeFleur's mouth, but it drowned in the blood filling his mouth.

Face down against the floor of the tunnel, he tried to push himself up. But there was neither strength nor feeling left in his arms. Helplessly, he watched his tormentor step over him and go after the others.

LeFleur's last sight was that of the Predator disappearing around the bend in the tunnel.

Andar waved Laban into the vehicle.

"Nice find," she said.

"Shut up and get in," he told her, keeping an eye on the stretch of tunnel behind them.

Mara was right behind Laban, his face looking pale and drawn, as if he had looked into the maw of hell. Emphalelo was already in the back seat, clutching a pistol to his chest and looking strangely wild-eyed.

But where was Broadhurst?

The lawyer had gone down one of the tunnels while Andar went down the other, both of them on foot. Having located as many of his comrades as he could, Andar had returned—thankfully, to a vehicle undiscovered by the Predators. But there was no sign of Broadhurst.

Just then, he heard the clatter of footfalls, and saw the lawyer pelt around a bend in the passage. "There's one behind us!" he cried out. "We've got to move!"

Us? Andar echoed silently.

A moment later, he saw Sildar make his way around the same bend, fighting a pronounced limp. His gray jumpsuit was torn and bloody, but he was moving. Halfway into the vehicle, Laban got out again and ran down the corridor to meet her employee.

Passing her, Broadhurst made a beeline for Andar. Without a moment's hesitation, he slid into the vehicle and thrust himself into the back seat next to Emphalelo.

Andar looked back at Laban and Sildar. They were taking too long. And if there was a Predator in pursuit . . .

Folding himself into the driver's seat, he manipulated the control that closed the doors. Then he backed down the tunnel until he reached Laban and Sildar—at which point he flipped the doors open again.

"Get going!" Sildar spat as he shoved Laban into the vehicle ahead of him.

A moment later, Andar saw why. Just behind them, the figure of a Predator had filled the tunnel. It was enormous and heavily armored, like all of its kind, and its shoulder cannon was emitting a red beam that found purchase in the rear portal of the humans' vehicle.

Andar swallowed. He had seen the aliens' plasma cannons at work. At this range, they wouldn't stand a chance against it. All the more reason to take off.

But he waited until Laban had dragged Sildar in after her. Then, as someone pulled the passenger's side door closed, Andar slammed the transmission into drive. It chugged to life and the machine began to move forward.

Andar dared to look back at their enemy, who was coming after them a stride at a time. But it was starting to fall behind. Soon they would be out of range of the Predator's weapon.

All it would take was a few seconds.

Come on, Andar urged, *get us out of here!*

A roar of fire came on the heels of his thought. Instinctively, he ducked. The white wave of energy swept over the vehicle—but it wasn't as powerful as it might have been. The increasing distance between the plasma cannon and its target had weakened its impact.

Still, the heat was tremendous. He could feel it inside the vehicle, and see it leave a coat of carbon dioxide over the rear portal. But they were in good shape.

Or so Andar thought, until the vehicle jerked a couple of times and slowed down.

"What the hell . . . ?" Laban growled.

"Give it a moment," Andar said, moving a control up into the red zone and hoping it was the right response.

The vehicle bucked again and again, but it couldn't seem to pick up speed. It was moving, but not quickly enough. Andar cursed and tried another control on his panel.

The rear monitor on his console showed him the Predator striding after them. But it wasn't firing. Did its plasma weapon need time between discharges?

"What's going on?" Laban demanded. "Can't we go any faster?"

"I'm doing my best," Andar snapped back at her, trying to remain calm despite the advance of the killing machine behind them.

At this rate, they would have to take another plasma blast. And another. And each one would bring them closer to being immobilized altogether.

Unless the plan Andar put in place bore some fruit, and quickly. Up ahead, not more than twenty feet away, he could see the rope he had strung across the width of the tunnel. It was low enough to escape the Predator's notice if they were lucky.

Just a little further, he thought.

Behind him, the Predator activated his red targeting beam. It found a hole in the charred surface of the vehicle's rear portal and thrust itself into their midst, an unwelcome invader. In a moment, the alien would blast away at them again. But a moment might be all Andar needed.

"Come on," he snarled from between clenched teeth.

Suddenly, the vehicle slowed down, as if it had were laboring under some excessive burden. At the same time, the tunnel filled with the sound of bending metal, responding to its torment with a shrill, high-pitched whine. Then there was a low rumble of rock, not from one place but from all around them.

Moments later, two steel rods that supported a section of the tunnel's ceiling were pulled out of place by the force of the vehicle's progress, and rocks began plummeting from above. Not just a few, either. The tunnel quickly filled with debris and dust—more than a ton of it, by Andar's estimate.

There was no way the Predator would be able to target them in such a mess. Or for that matter, follow them.

The vehicle, its heavy work done, began to move freely again, carrying them deeper into the mountain—and further away from the Predators.

Mara looked surprised as he turned to Andar. "You knew that would happen?"

"I *hoped* it would happen," Andar corrected him. "I planned on it. But I didn't know for sure."

Mara looked back through their rear portal at the stretch of tunnel behind them. Andar knew he would find no sign of the Predator in the rolling cloud of pulverized-stone dust.

"I'm glad it worked out for you," Mara said without inflection.

TEN

The argument was an unpleasant one. Bet-Karh congratulated himself on his self-restraint; another Hunter might have struck Heith-Rek with a boulder by now.

Heith-Rek, one of the two Hunters in the party from Kirs-Giras's clan, had seen some of the humans retreat into this tunnel and had given pursuit. However, the humans had had a vehicle waiting for them, and had arranged a rock collapse to block the Hunters' way. Heith-Rek had been injured in the collapse, but not so much that he couldn't continue the Hunt.

In fact, the injury to Kaj-Nal's thigh was worse. But he didn't want to give up either. Like Heith-Rek, he insisted that they clear the tunnel and go after the humans. But then, it was the way of their clan—the one led by Kirs-Garas—to meet problems head-on.

Bet-Karh, on the other hand, wanted to extract his hunting party from the mountain and circle around to trap the humans on the other side.

They already knew from their scans that there were only three tunnel mouths on the far side of the mountain. The debris blocking the tunnel was considerable, and—though hardly beyond the capabilities of four Hish—would take some time to clear. And the tunnel mouth by which they had entered the mountain was not so far away.

It seemed to Bet-Karh that there was only one logical course of action. But as he had learned in the past, the logic of his clan was not necessarily the logic of Kirs-Garas's clan.

Heith-Rek repeated his contention that the direct approach was the better one, the approach that resulted in the greatest number of kills. His clan had always hunted this way. To do otherwise would be to dishonor his ancestors.

Bet-Karh reminded Heith-Rek that Bet-Karh's people had traditions as well—and that theirs required a more measured method of taking down prey. To Bet-Karh's clan, a desperate target was a target that might turn and inflict unnecessary damage. The humans had already demonstrated their capacity to do so with their collapse of the tunnel ceiling. There was no telling what other tricks they might have in mind.

The Hunt, said Bet-Karh, was not a slaughter. It was a chase, a game, a battle of wits. The true Hunter employed stealth and cunning to snare his prey. Anything less was unseemly.

Heith-Rek and his clanmate scoffed at Bet-Karh's words. That is a dance, they said, not a Hunt.

Normally, Bet-Karh would have met the insult with bloodshed. It was all he could do to refrain from it, and to remind the others that their leaders wanted this Hunt to be a joint effort—the beginning of melding the two clans into one. It meant both sides had to find ways to work together, to accomplish their goals, and to learn from one another.

Heith-Rek fell silent, as if daring Bet-Karh to come up with a plan that would straddle their differences. His body language said he was ready to hunt, to pursue the humans who had scurried into the mountain's scars like insects seeking the hive. But he gave Bet-Karh a chance to respond.

Bet-Karh looked at Heith-Rek, and then at the others in turn. He couldn't take long to ponder their next move. Each moment he deliberated, their prey would get further away.

As he pondered his options, he heard a buzzing noise—one he had heard before. Whipping his head around, he spotted—with the help of his helmet's magnification function—an airborne machine at the furthest point in the tunnel. It appeared to be watching them.

Surveillance of some sort? Bet-Karh wondered.

He manipulated the controls of his plasma weapon, narrowing its focus, and then activated the targeting mechanism. Despite the fact that the airborne device was in motion, his training allowed him to maintain a target lock. He eased the trigger and a single shot of pure energy leaped out along the tunnel, obliterating the device.

If the machine were indeed a surveillance device, it seemed likely that some form of counter-attack was imminent. The Hunters were best off cloaking, in that case. But first, he needed to lay out his plan—for Bet-Karh had finally formulated one.

ELEVEN

Andar and his party hadn't gone very far in their borrowed vehicle before the lighting ahead of them flickered and went off. As he slowed the vehicle's progress to a crawl, he wondered if the tunnel collapse he had engineered was in some way related to the lighting failure. He wouldn't have been the least bit surprised.

Fumbling with his controls, Andar found the one that activated the vehicle's headlights. As they blinked on, the first sight that greeted him was a huge stalactite. Behind it were other stalactites, a haphazard assortment of them.

Whoever had dug this tunnel had clearly broken into some caverns formed by underwater streams in the mountain. The floor, fortunately, was free of stalagmites, or they might have had a problem. As it was, they just had a nicer view.

Accelerating again, Andar spotted emergency lighting fixtures that were obviously no longer in service. There was no other evidence that the miners had been there. Their path seemed straight, without obstruction, but he wished he had some idea where they were going and where they might find an exit.

His companions were craning their necks around, studying the cavern in childlike awe. A silence had fallen over them, each no doubt occupied with the same thoughts that preoccupied Andar. *How many Predators are there? Where are they now? Will we ever get out of here alive?*

He only wished he had answers for them.

Laban was leaning forward, taking in the scenery. She seemed to sense that he was looking at her and glanced back. She looked tired and worn, even more so than the others. None of them had had any food or water in hours, and they had all lost comrades.

But Laban's burden was different. She was the one in charge. Whatever weighed on the others weighed twice as hard on her.

"Those Predators," she said, "are something."

It was a monumental understatement. "It feels," said Andar, "like they've sent elephants to stomp on ants."

"The heat they're packing . . ." she said, her voice trailing off.

He nodded, turning back to the path ahead of them. "I'm convinced now that Derek is behind this. He's always been about overkill."

"Well, this is as much overkill as I can imagine."

They rode on in silence. Eventually, their path began to curve and slope down. On either side of his vehicle, Andar could see the handiwork of countless miners—steel supports, evenly matched scratches in the walls, a choice bit of graffiti here and there. But nothing they could turn into weapons, no emergency communications equipment, no signs of life.

The path leveled off again and in the distance, Andar spotted the pinprick that he always heard about: the light at the end of the tunnel. It grew, and the others seemed to spot it as well.

Some fifty feet from the entrance, Andar depressed the brake with his foot, slowing them down. All the while, the light waxed larger, more inviting—especially after the gloom and close confinement of the tunnels. Finally, he brought them to a complete stop.

In the light of day, Andar turned to the others—Laban, Broadhurst, Mara, Sildar, and Emphalelo—and saw how dirty, bruised, and bloodied they all were. No one's clothing was intact, and only Sildar looked like he was fully alert.

"Why don't we keep going?" asked Broadhurst. "We're not out of here yet."

"No," Laban conceded, "but we have to get quiet. For all we know, they have Predators at every tunnel mouth."

"Then we hie ourselves home," said Mara. "Unfortunately, it looks like we'll be late for the reading of the will."

Andar didn't respond to the remark. He wasn't looking forward to the reading before and he certainly wasn't now—though he wanted to make it just to see Derek's face. No doubt, his cousin would be surprised that he had survived.

You haven't survived yet, a voice in his head reminded him.

Dousing the lights in the vehicle, he got out and watched the others follow suit. By the time Emphalelo emerged, leaving the vehicle empty, Laban was inching along the tunnel wall to get a glimpse of what was waiting for them outside.

"What's out there?' asked Broadhurst, his voice little more than a croak.

"Nothing," Laban breathed, using a hand to shade her eyes against the sunlight.

But then, the Predators weren't going to give themselves away so easily. They might be in hiding, waiting only for the humans to come out before they began blasting away.

And if that were so, there would be little they could do about it. They were all armed, but their weapons had proven pretty ineffectual against the aliens' armor.

Laban went so far as to stick her head outside the tunnel. Nothing shot at her. Nothing buzzed. In fact, nothing happened at all.

A good sign, Andar thought.

But it was hardly an assurance of safety. They all knew that. Even Broadhurst, who might never have done anything more dangerous than plug in a maser oven.

Andar felt sorry for getting the attorney mixed up in this. But then, Broadhurst had worked for Gregor Ciejek, and then for Grandpa Karl. He hadn't gone into his duties blindly. He had to know there was a measure of risk.

"Hey," said Laban, "look at this." And she took a step out into the sunlight.

Andar followed her, feeling the sun sting his sweaty face with its heat. As the tableau opened in front of him, he found himself looking down on a plateau full of mining equipment. The table of land was maybe a hundred yards in diameter, with dark, barren slopes rising steeply from the other sides of it.

Some of the smaller pieces of equipment looked too rusted to be of use to anyone. However, there were three big pieces that seemed to be in reasonably good shape.

One was a huge, bright yellow excavation device, one of the machines designed to chew through the exterior of the mountain and expose raw minerals for collection. Another was a squat, indestructible-looking old-style dump truck. The third was something that dwarfed everything around it, a tremendous orange and gray vehicle that featured a gigantic bucket wheel and an arsenal of drills.

Andar estimated that he could stand in any of those buckets and not be seen. The machine had twelve crawlers, eight in front and four in the back. He couldn't even begin to estimate its height or width.

"Any idea what this is?" he asked.

"Yes," said Laban. "Your grandfather talked about it a while back. It digs holes in mountains."

By then, some of the others had joined them at the tunnel mouth. Broadhurst put his hand on Andar's shoulder and said, "Mother of God . . ."

"A neighborhood could move into that thing," Mara quipped.

Now that Andar knew what it did, he could see the machine's handiwork in the chewed-up sections of mountain behind it.

The slopes looked as if gigantic scoops had been taken out of them from midway down to the ground. Andar could only imagine how much earth the thing could move, how powerful it could be. Something that size might even withstand a plasma blast or three.

It might also be able to get them out of there. Not by going over the mountains, but by going *through* them. Andar shared his observation with the others.

"Hey," said Mara, "whatever works."

"We're about ten clicks from the colony," Sildar noted. "And that thing doesn't look like it's built for speed."

"Once we're free of the mountains," said Andar, "we can get out and walk. But if it's as durable as it looks, we may want to stay inside it."

"Think it has any juice left?" Broadhurst asked.

"Maybe," said Laban.

"I'm going to go check it out," said Andar.

"Why you?" asked Laban, giving him a look.

He shrugged. "Why not?"

Laban considered him for a moment. Then she turned to Sildar and said, "Cover him."

The security chief nodded.

Taking that as his cue, Andar moved away from the tunnel mouth and approached the giant machine. As he did so, he searched the mountain slopes for indications of the aliens' presence. He didn't find any.

But if Broadhurst was right, they could bend light about themselves and hide in plain view. If that were true, he wouldn't see them until it was too late.

A comforting thought.

He had gotten halfway to the machine when he saw a movement out of the corner of his eye. Whirling, he tried to figure out exactly where it had come from. But he couldn't.

And there wasn't any ensuing blast of destructive energy. In fact, there was nothing at all.

Andar wiped some sweat from his brow. *Am I seeing things?* he asked himself. He wouldn't have been the first human being in history to suffer from paranoia.

In this case, it was justified. But as nothing had happened, he continued his progress. Less than a minute later, he reached the machine. Up close it looked even bigger, more imposing.

Nothing jumped out at him to suggest a power source. But there was a cockpit, hidden from the tunnel mouth so he hadn't noticed it before. And there were handholds and inset ladders that would enable him to scale the thing.

Taking advantage of them, he clambered up and inserted himself into the cockpit.

It was even hotter inside than it was outside. *Like being in an oven*, Andar thought. But he focused on the colossus' control panel, not knowing how much time he would have to figure it out.

Fortunately, he had had some experience working with heavy machinery back on Earth, clearing radioactive-waste sites. Not for a long time, but long enough to know how big machines operated. In a matter of seconds, he had sussed out the controls.

But as he had feared, there was no power in the thing's batteries. It was stone cold dead, like some prehistoric behemoth.

However, if there were batteries, there had to be a power source to charge them—and it had to be somewhere nearby. All they had to do was find it and they could power the machine back up.

That was the theory, anyway. In fact, the machine might have other problems. But they wouldn't know that for certain until they found the power source.

Andar leaned out of the cockpit and gestured for the others to join him. One by one, they filed out of the tunnel, a couple of them walking backwards so they could spot signs of pursuit.

"We've got to find a power line," he told Laban, "to charge this thing's batteries. Otherwise, it's not moving an inch."

"Done," said Laban, and passed the word on.

As his comrades spread out to look for the line, Andar took advantage of his higher vantage point to scan the plateau for the aliens. If they were cloaked, would they cast shadows? Maybe not.

But the ground there was dry and dusty. Every so often, a breeze kicked up a dirty brown cloud. If a Predator were caught in it, he would be exposed.

He, Andar thought. *As if I have any idea what sex they are, or if they even have sexes the way we do.* The truth was they could all have been females.

He didn't know how many of them were actually involved. As far as he could tell, there were only a handful in the tunnel— the same amount they had encountered in the forest. But there could have been a lot more of them in the area.

Andar was still looking for signs of the aliens when he saw something hovering in the distance—something cylindrical and metallic-looking, peeking past an outcropping of rock directly above the tunnel mouth. He would never have noticed it were it not for his vantage point and the glint of sunshine on its surface.

It was the thing he had glimpsed before. It had to be. But what was it? A spy device? Something the aliens used to track their prey?

I'd better alert the others, he thought, and slid himself out of the cockpit.

"What's the matter?" Laban asked him as he dropped to the ground.

"Don't turn around," he said, "but I think we're being watched. I saw something metallic hovering behind that jut of rock just over the tunnel."

Laban's brow knotted over the bridge of her delicate nose. "I'll take care of it. You get back up there."

So when they found the power source, he could start the machine without delay. He understood, and headed back for the machine.

He had barely begun to climb when he heard the shriek of tortured metal behind him. Casting a look back over his shoulder, he saw something go clanking down the slope beside the tunnel mouth.

It hit the ground hard and noisily, and lay there on its side. As far as Andar could tell, it had been disabled—whatever it was.

Mara was the first to reach it. He picked it up—inadvisably, perhaps—and inspected it. By the time Andar and the others joined him, he was nodding.

"What?" asked Laban.

"I've seen this before," said Mara.

Laban looked at him askance. "You've been hanging out with Predators and not telling me?"

"It's not a Predator device," Mara replied. "It's an airborne drone with camera and transmission ability, made in Australia back on Earth."

"And you say you saw it before?" Andar asked.

Mara turned to him and seemed to hesitate. "Back at the compound. The morning of the day your father died."

Sildar snapped his fingers. "That's right. I remember now. We shot at it and it got away."

Laban nodded. "Right. And we wondered who was behind it—which other syndicate. But I would never have recognized it."

"There's another possibility," said Andar. "That it was Derek's."

"Why do you say that?" asked Emphalelo.

"I grew up with that twisted son of a bitch," said Andar. "He always liked to watch things from a distance. Especially other people's pain."

He remembered one time when they were very young and Derek set a trap for his father. There was a walking path just outside the compound, which Bela liked to use for his morning constitutionals. It got narrow in one particular spot, where it wound its way around a boulder.

Derek dug a hole and covered it with twigs and leaves, as if he were trying to catch a wild animal. Then he asked Andar to come watch something with him. Not knowing what he was watching, Andar hunkered down in the woods—and saw Bela twist his ankle.

As he cried out in pain, he saw the boys take off. Afterward, as he limped around with the help of a cane, he advised Gregor to give Andar a whipping. Derek, on the other hand, got off with nothing more than some advice: to steer clear of Andar, who was obviously a bad influence.

Derek would have liked nothing more than to watch his uncle fade. It made Andar boil inside to think about it.

"It was Derek," he said. "Trust me."

Then something else occurred to him.

What if Derek hadn't just been enjoying Gregor's pain? What if he was the one who had caused it?

Gregor's death hadn't seemed suspicious. But it was a wide galaxy, and men were discovering new kinds of drugs all the time. How hard would it have been for Derek to administer one of those drugs to Gregor and send him sliding toward death?

Derek wanted control of the family, and had since well before Andar left. Who had stood in the way of that? Gregor. Grandpa Karl. And despite his absence, Andar.

First dad died, then Grandpa Karl, and now I'm running for my life from a pack of alien über-hunters. Coincidence? Andar didn't think so.

If the drone belonged to Derek, he had to know what had become of Andar and his party—had to know what kind of trouble they were in. And yet, there was no sign of help.

Because Derek was the one who had planned their deaths, and then sent out a drone so he could watch. It all began to make sense, in a bizarre and bloody way.

The Ciejeks hadn't needed any enemies to destroy them. They'd had an enemy right in their own midst.

Andar turned to Laban. "Do you think there's any way dad was killed? Poisoned to death?"

She seemed surprised by the question—and more than a little indignant. "Don't you think I would have known it?"

"Not necessarily," he said.

Putting aside her resentment, she seemed to consider the possibility more seriously. "It *was* a baffling illness. The doctors didn't seem to know how to treat him. And he didn't want an autopsy . . ."

"So you never understood how he got sick," said Andar.

Laban looked at him. "You . . . you think Derek had something to do with Gregor's death?"

Andar nodded. "Damned right I do. Why else would he have had a drone watching my father—except to make sure nothing would go wrong? So he could take the first step in seizing control of the family?"

They all stood there in the hot sun, absorbing the remark, coming to grips with the idea of who their real enemy might be. Not the Predators, but Derek Ciejek.

Sildar's face twisted into a mask of hatred. "I'll kill the motherfucker."

"After *me*," Andar said.

But first, they had to escape the alien hunters, who—by virtue of their cloaking technology—might be standing beside them at that very moment.

It was Broadhurst who finally gave them hope. "I see something that might be the power conduit," he called out.

He jabbed a finger at something long and snakelike but very, very thick, coiled under one of the machine's mammoth treads. If it still had any juice, they might be able to coax the colossus to life.

"Where do we plug it in?" Broadhurst asked, scrutinizing the machine.

"Somewhere near the end of the cable," Laban said, a hint of disdain in her voice.

It took another moment to find the place where the cable was to be inserted. Then, together, the six of them wrestled the heavy cable out of its coils and plugged the end of it into the machine.

"Thank God," Broadhurst muttered when they were done.

"God has got nothing to do with this mess," Sildar snapped.

They didn't know where the other end of the cable went, or the nature of the power source they would find there. But it didn't really matter, if it did the job.

Climbing back into the cockpit, Andar checked the power gauges. Sure enough, they were registering an energy intake. But it wasn't going to happen all at once. It would take time.

And with the Predators most assuredly on their trail, time was a precious commodity.

Trying to ignore the heat and the inevitable arrival of the aliens, Andar gave the engines time to charge. *Come on*, he thought, watching the gauge.

It was moving ever so slowly. At that rate, it would take twenty minutes to charge fully. But they probably wouldn't be able to wait that long.

Then we'll stay here as long as we can, he decided, *and hope for the best*.

Laban had already started directing the others into the buckets. Making use of the handholds and ladders on the sides of the machine, they climbed into one scoop or another. Only Sildar remained on the ground, his weapon at the ready, intent on covering his companions until they were secure.

Finally, when Broadhurst was about halfway to his assigned bucket, Sildar tucked his weapon away, grabbed a handhold, and began his own climb.

"They're coming!" someone cried out.

It was Laban. She was standing up in her bucket, pointing to a spot on the slope of the mountain from which they had emerged.

At first, Andar didn't see anything. Then a couple of Predators shimmered into view, their plasma weapons already a fiery red. Before anyone could make a move, the aliens fired. Their plasma bursts struck the machine and splattered, sending a shiver through the metal. But as far as Andar could tell, the attack didn't damage anything.

Then Sildar, who was still standing at the base of the machine so his companions could get into the buckets, fired back.

His shots were true. They struck one of the Predators, then the other. But all the impacts did was slow them down a little—and alert them to the fact that he was a threat.

As Andar watched helplessly, the aliens took aim again and fired. This time, their blasts raked Sildar like birds of prey, turning him into a fireball as they drove him backwards into the machine.

No . . . ! Andar screamed inside.

He could have leaped from the cockpit and gone to the weapons master's aid, but that would have left the others at the mercy of the Predators—like clams in metal shells, waiting to be pried out of them. Besides, he doubted that Sildar was still alive.

But *someone* went to Sildar's aid. With a cry, Laban vaulted over the side of her bucket and dropped to the ground. Even before she hit the surface, she was firing at the Predators.

One of her shots found a target, bringing the alien up short. But the other hunter returned the barrage with one of its own.

Only the edge of the plasma beam made contact with Laban—but that was more than enough to make her left arm burst into flame, the force of the blast sending her spinning to the ground. In the next breath, the Predator advanced on her, preparing to fire again.

Andar pulled his weapon out, leaned out of the cockpit, and squeezed off an energy volley. But his aim was erratic. The Predator just kept coming, and a moment later the other Predator started advancing again as well.

Somehow, Laban got back to her feet and stumbled in the direction of the digging machine. But the Predators were faster than she was, and they had already proven that they could nail her with a plasma blast. Left to her own devices, she was a dead woman.

Andar started to climb out of the cockpit, heedless of the consequences. Then he stopped—and realized he had a better option, one that was more likely to save Laban's life.

Though the engines hadn't charged as much as he would have liked, he pressed the stud that activated them. Instantly, he felt energy surge through the digging machine, only a subtle thrum at first. Then the vibrations grew more powerful, bringing the mechanical colossus back to life.

At the same time, the Predators were bearing down on Laban. They could have fired at her and finished her off from a distance, but they had refrained—maybe so they could do so in a slower, more painful way. It made Andar feel sick to think so.

But they weren't going to get Laban. Not if he could help it.

He waited until the aliens were almost on top of Laban, their attention riveted on her. Then he punched another stud in his control panel and manipulated the pressure-sensitive ring around it.

Before the Predators knew what was happening, a very long, very sharp drill extended toward them on a multi-jointed metal arm, and whirred to life. One of them moved quickly enough to throw himself to the ground, but the other wasn't so fortunate.

With a high-pitched whine, the drill buried itself in the alien's chest, ripping apart its armor and sending viscera flying in every direction. The Predator jerked a few times like a rag doll on a string, then slumped backward.

Reversing the spin of the drill, Andar extracted it from its victim. His intention was to go after the other Predator with it, to do to that one what he had done to the first.

But his intended target had already taken the offensive, taking aim with its plasma weapon. Its first shot missed but its second struck the drill, breaking off a piece. What remained still whirred at a dizzying speed, striking at the alien like a basilisk.

But the Predator was too quick for it. Ducking and rolling, it came up firing. A second time, it took a piece out of the drill with a plasma barrage. Again the drill darted at the alien, and again he eluded it.

Despite the raw power of the drill, the hunter was quicker and more agile. In time, the drill would be destroyed, and the Predator would be free to seek another target.

Worse, two other Predators were swimming into view at the far side of the plateau, their weapons pointed at the machine. Now Andar had three adversaries to contend with. But if all went well, he wouldn't have to contend with them for long.

Because Mara and Emphalelo had taken advantage of the distraction to leap to the ground and recover Laban. At that very moment, they were pulling her up along the side of the machine to deposit her in one of the buckets.

They had chosen to leave Sildar. No doubt, he was beyond their help.

Andar struggled with the controls, battling the Predator in front of him. *Just a few more moments*, he thought, a bead of perspiration rolling down the side of his face, *and we can get out of here. Just a few more moments . . .*

The broken drill jabbed at the Predator, nearly pinning it to the ground. But the hunter rolled away in time, then opened fire at close range. The machine vibrated with the force of the attack and, to Andar's dismay, the drill stopped spinning.

He cursed to himself. But by then, everyone was safe in one of the buckets—Laban included. They could make their getaway.

The two newly arrived aliens leveled a couple of blasts at the digging machine, causing it to shiver a little. But it remained intact. And before they could do any more damage, Andar swung it around.

The machine was faster than he might have guessed. He didn't know exactly which way they had to go, but he had a general idea. Pouring on the power, he sent the thing trundling toward a rocky slope.

A deafening sound filled his ears as the machine's myriad drills went to work pulverizing rock, dirt, and vegetation. It was the sound of destruction, the sound of age-old bonds being torn asunder. But for Andar and his surviving companions, it was also the sound of freedom.

No doubt the Predators were firing at them, trying to hobble them and stop them from getting away. But as the machine plowed into the mountainside, it pushed piles of debris into its wake. And as they built up, they became bulwarks against the aliens' plasma bursts.

Had Andar been able to deploy the buckets, he could have expedited the process. But with his comrades hunkered down in some of them, he didn't have that option.

Before his eyes, the mountain fell away, layer by tough, resistant layer. The piles of debris behind him grew more and more numerous. And the Predators, despite their tenacity, were gradually left behind.

Finally, even the brilliance of their plasma blasts disappeared. They were history. Andar felt a little jolt of satisfaction.

But his job wasn't done yet. He still had to try to keep Laban alive. And when that was accomplished, he intended to make his cousin Derek pay for what he had done.

TWELVE

The views on the multiple-screen setup had stopped enter-taining Derek Ciejek some time earlier—and for good reason. Somehow, against any odds worth betting on, his cousin had avoided destruction at the hands of the Predators.

With morbid fascination, Derek had watched as the aliens left the forest and traced the humans to the mountain. He had cheered out loud as each of Andar's men was taken down, one after the other. He hadn't left his seat for a moment, reluctant to miss even a single small act of mutilation.

Marlene and his other employees had drifted in and out of his cabin, incapable of sharing his lust for mayhem. Snacks had been brought to him so he wouldn't have to get up. He concen-trated strictly on switching drone angles, looking for the most satisfying and entertaining perspective on the bloodshed.

The drones' signals had become more garbled the deeper they went into the mountain, but Derek hadn't left his seat then either. He could still make out what was happening, so he hung in. Such was his hunger for violence.

He didn't like it when the Predators spotted one of the drones and destroyed it. However, that was a risk he had assumed from the beginning. Besides, with nearly a dozen other drones still in operation, there would be plenty for him to see.

Then matters had gotten out of hand.

He had actually begun screaming at the screens when the Predators allowed their human prey—Andar among them—to board the mining machine. Briefly, his fury had turned to glee when Laban was clipped with a plasma burst. But before long, he had plenty of reason to get angry again, as the mining machine began to dig a hole through the mountain . . .

And kept going until it was out of sight.

Grabbing a glass, Derek hurled it at one of the screens as hard as he could. On impact, both glass and screen shattered in an explosion of jagged shards.

"Stupid son of a *bitch*!" he shrieked at his cousin.

"He was never stupid, sweetie," came the unexpected reply.

Whirling in his chair, Derek saw Marlene standing in the doorway. "Whose side are you on?" he demanded.

"Yours, of course," she told him. "Which is why I'm reminding you of the truth. Your cousin's not stupid."

"Okay, if you're so damned smart—where's he headed now?"

"To the reading of the will. After all, he's got a reason now to claim his share—and you're it."

"What? He doesn't know I'm behind any of this."

"Oh," said Marlene, "he knows, all right. Did you see his expression change when he was talking with the others—right after he shot down one of your drones? He went from fear to suspicion to hatred in a matter of moments. Trust me—he knows."

Derek swore beneath his breath.

He hadn't imagined that Andar would ever live long enough to attend the reading of the will. He had just assumed that the family fortune was his alone—not just after he sprang his trap on Andar, but long before.

Which was why he had made deals with other syndicates. Deals he couldn't renege on, or he would have them all breathing down his neck like a pack of hungry dogs. Derek styled himself as a badass, but there were far badder asses out there, and he didn't want any of them angry with him.

"Doesn't matter," he said. "The Predators will catch up with him eventually."

"I don't believe that," said Marlene. "And if I know you even a little bit, neither do you."

The way she said it made him want to smack her. Smack her *hard*. But if he started hitting his second, his men would take note of it. Their loyalty would be eroded. And right now, that was the last thing he needed.

"They might not even follow Andar as far as the colony," said Marlene. "I don't think they expected to take on anything that big. They may turn around and leave. Who can say?"

Derek's hands were shaking, he was so angry. Andar should have been dead. He should have been history.

I have to do something, Derek told himself. Hoping for inspiration, he flicked from one drone to the next, using his three remaining screens. Unfortunately, they didn't show him anything that changed the cold, hard truth.

Finally, a course of action floated to the surface, one he didn't necessarily like but one that worked for him. He toggled off the screens and got to his feet. His meaty right hand hit a different kind of control, and he addressed the microphone that lit up beside him.

"Pack your hardware and get to the shuttle bay," he told his men. "We're going back down. And we're on a schedule, so hustle."

Flipping the control off, he turned and stared at Marlene, who hadn't budged from the doorway. He arched an eyebrow at her and she returned the stare.

"Coming?" he asked. "I did say we're on a schedule."

"I want to know what you have planned."

"Simple. We go down there, meet Andar and his people before they get to the reading, and kill everyone in sight."

Marlene didn't bat an eyelash. "That might work. What about your friends, the Predators?"

"We avoid them," Derek said with an annoyance in his voice he hadn't intended. "We make the hit, I inherit everything, we get back up here—and then we go home."

"You intend to *avoid* those aliens?" Marlene made it sound ludicrous. "They have a ship, too. They can follow us."

"You have a better plan?" he asked. His anger was flaming hotter, and he was afraid he might smack her one after all.

"I'm saying you're acting impulsively," she returned. "I'm saying you can't leave a loose end like the Predators on Felicity."

He could hear the footsteps up and down the decks as his team assembled their gear. "We're on a cruiser," he spat, "not a battle ship. I can't blow them out of the sky, and I doubt most of our weapons will hurt them close up."

"I *hate* loose ends," she said, staying on her point.

He owed her much of his success. He needed her. That was all that kept him from killing her.

"I got a situation here," he said, forcing calm into his voice. "I gotta fix it, starting with Andar. Then I can figure something out with the Predators."

"You'll have maybe twenty minutes, and that's about it," she said, and left the room to get ready.

Derek watched her go, his hands opening and closing in spasms of fury. It took a while before his anger abated enough for him to compose himself and go to his cabin to get his gear.

Along the way, he passed three of his men, hurrying forward. One, Turgeon, was fastening a vest pocket straining to contain the spare cartridges he had jammed into it.

They all paused as he approached, but Derek waved them on. Continuing to his sleeping quarters, he allowed the door to close behind him. Then he went to the sink and splashed water on his face. He wanted to make sure he looked calm and collected, a leader who didn't fear a thing—especially his cousin.

He next pulled a case from a slot under his bed and snapped it open, using his thumbprint to activate the locking mechanism. Nestled inside the case were several pistols of varying vintage as well as firepower. He grabbed them all and the magazines for each.

Derek admired each weapon in turn. The first, an old-style 9mm Glock, he tucked into a hip pocket. The second, a high-powered energy pistol, he slipped into the other hip pocket. There really wasn't a good place for the third, an advanced-prototype TASER he got through someone who owed him a favor.

Fortunately, he had a shoulder holster in his luggage. It took but seconds to retrieve it and slip it over his shoulders. As he did this, he thought back to when his Grandpa Karl gave it to him as a birthday gift. How old was he? Seventeen? Eighteen?

Derek had cherished it, keeping it well oiled and maintained. He always brought it with him on trips, a talisman for good fortune. The TASER fit neatly into the holster.

Finally, Derek grabbed a knife in its leather sheath and snaked it through his belt, making certain he could walk without it slapping against him. If there was even a chance of his seeing a Predator, he wanted every advantage—though he wasn't sure even his armor-piercing bullets would get through the alien junk they wore. He wished he had a small tactical nuke, just to be safe.

Not that he would be alone. His men would be armed as well. And they would outnumber what was left of Andar's entourage. His cousin would be drastically overmatched and outgunned.

But then, it wasn't Andar he was afraid of.

Quickly, Derek made his way to the shuttle bay. When he arrived, he saw that the others had beaten him there.

Ibrahim, dark and angular as an obsidian dagger, was in the pilot's chair, already running the pre-flight checklist. Marlene was sitting beside him, reviewing the navigation charts, seeking the landing port that would put them closest to the site of the reading.

Fortunately, the colony wasn't all that big. Someone had nicknamed it "Mayberry" after a town from an old television series. He had agreed with the assessment when he arrived for that sham of a dinner.

Was that really only yesterday?

He settled in, strapped himself to the chair, and gave Marlene a thumbs-up. Moments later, the door was sealed and the airlock was emptied of atmosphere.

Less than twenty minutes after Derek had determined that he needed to be on the planet's surface, he was leading his team of ten men and one woman into what he imagined would be a final confrontation with Andar's side of the family.

Felicity, seen through gaps in the dirty white cloud cover, gleamed in golden sunlight as the shuttle descended. Derek smiled to himself. He and his men were armed and ready. With just a little luck, they would be back aboard his ship before its next orbit was completed.

THIRTEEN

Kneeling over his fallen comrade and the gaping wound in his chest, Bet-Karh took a moment to honor him silently. No doubt, he reflected, Kaj-Nal would have protected himself better if he hadn't taken that wound to his thigh back in the tunnels.

The humans had acquitted themselves better than Bet-Karh would have guessed. More than half of them had been claimed by the hunting party, but the rest had escaped in the digging machine. Their pack leader, whoever he was, was worthy of Bet-Karh's respect.

Slaying him would make the young hunter happy indeed.

He looked up at the two other Hish, who looked back at him expectantly. The air above them was thick with dirt, the sky a light brown instead of deep blue. They couldn't be pleased by the way things had turned out. The Hunt-lust was still with them, unsatisfied, just as it was with Bet-Karh.

Worse, he would soon have to report to the clan leaders, and he wasn't looking forward to that conversation. He needed to have something positive to tell them, something that would meet with their approval.

But it wouldn't be easy to catch the humans. Though Bet-Karh could still hear the high-pitched whine of the machine's drills and the rumbling protests of the mountain, he couldn't see the machine any longer. It had left too much earth and crushed rock behind it.

The hunting party would need forever to clear away that much debris. As with the cave-in back in the tunnel, it made more sense to take a different approach, to go around or over the obstacles in front of them.

Of course, Heith-Rek would believe otherwise. In keeping with his clan's philosophy, he would want to follow the machine into the mountain, no matter how patently stupid the strategy might be.

In the tunnel, Bet-Karh had insisted on continuing the Hunt his way, and had won out. Now, with Heith-Rek's clan-mate gone, Heith-Rek might be defensive—and therefore less tractable. So Bet-Karh took a different approach—and asked Heith-Rek what he thought their next move should be.

Heith-Rek was surprised that he was being asked. That much was evident in his posture. It was also clear that he was feeling less adversarial—exactly the result Bet-Karh had hoped for when he made the overture.

Suddenly, a shrill sound filled Bet-Karh's helmet, signaling an incoming message from the Hish ship. Bet-Karh was relieved that it was just a message, and not the clan leaders themselves. He held his hand up for silence so he could hear.

A moment later, the recorded voice of Dre-Nath filled the hunter's helmet. Apparently, a small human-made vessel had left its mother vessel in orbit, and was descending in the direc-tion of the human colony. It would land just ten miles from the hunters' current position.

Dre-Nath believed that the vessel's deployment was a response to the hunters' presence. He wanted Bet-Karh to know that he was sending additional hunters to the vicinity. Like the other three, Dre-Nath noted, they would report to Bet-Karh. Then the message ended.

Absorbing the information, Bet-Karh found himself comforted by the quickness and decisiveness of the clan's move—an indication that the two leaders were working well together on the ship. If they were to survive, they would have to build on this new spirit of cooperation and unity.

Bet-Karh eyed his remaining comrades and passed on what he had heard. Their priority, he said, had to be the newcomers in the arriving vessel, as they were likely to be more formidable than the humans they had faced so far. The prey in the digging machine could be attended to later.

There was nothing Andar wanted at that moment more than a drink of water.

His cousin's heart on a platter was high on his wish list as well. But water . . . ? He would have killed for it. Literally.

As he had feared, the digging machine died on them. First it did its job, getting them through the mountain and within a few miles of the colony. But its batteries hadn't had time to charge fully, and Andar had asked a lot of it. So he wasn't shocked when the drills stopped drilling, and the treads stopped moving, and the machine finally froze in its tracks, forcing them to continue on foot.

They were taking turns carrying Laban on a makeshift stretcher made from their shirts and a couple of saplings they had cut down. Emphalelo, who knew a little about first aid, had managed to cauterize her wound and stop the bleeding, but Laban was in shock. If they didn't get her to a doctor soon, she would die.

But then, with the Predators after them, they all stood a chance of that.

No one commented on the heat—not Mara, not Emphalelo, and not Broadhurst. Andar scanned the horizon. There was no sign of the colony yet, but it was out there. Any minute, it would make an appearance.

Withdrawing his cellular from his pocket, he tried to get a signal—and failed. But he saw by the device's clock that it was mid-afternoon. At this rate, he would never make it to the reading of the will in time.

He laughed a harsh, throaty laugh, drawing stares from the others. He didn't care. The will seemed so meaningless in the context of everything that had happened.

The pain. The bloodshed. He would gladly have given away his inheritance for a cool glass of water, were it not for one thing—the satisfaction Derek would have derived from seeing his cousin out of the picture.

In a way, that was all that kept Andar going. That and the knowledge that Katarina was waiting for him back on Earth. She wouldn't be happy if he died there on Felicity. Not at all. Half-giddy with the heat, he wished he could call the lawyers presiding over the reading and let them know he would be late. He could just imagine the conversation . . .

"Keefer, Scheeler, and Palmer. How may I direct your call?"

"Heather Scheeler, please. It's Andar Ciejek."

"One moment, please."

"Of course."

"Hi, Mr. Ciejek. This is Heather Scheeler. Are we still on for four?"

"Probably not, Ms. Scheeler. You see, I've got a little problem . . ."

Andar shook his head and kept walking.

After a while, he saw a vessel against the hard, deep blue of the sky. It was descending in the direction of the colony. But it didn't look like anything he had seen on the ship that brought him there.

From some other ship, then, he concluded, his thoughts slow and murky like an underground river. *A commercial vessel? Or maybe . . . Derek's ship?*

Was it coming to take Derek off the planet? His heart sank in his chest. Once Derek got back to the family compound, Andar would never be able to get to him. He had to do so there on Felicity, or not at all.

He concentrated all his attention on the small craft and where it was likely to land. If he got to it before Derek did, he could surprise its pilot and use it to get Laban to a doctor. Then he could find Derek and settle their score.

Finally, the craft fell out of sight. But Andar saw where it had crossed the horizon. He made an adjustment and headed in that direction.

"Where are you going?" Broadhurst asked, trying to catch up with Andar.

"Did you see that craft?" Andar asked him.

Broadhurst looked shell-shocked. But then, he was accustomed to clean offices and expense-account lunches. If ever there was a fish out of water in that place, it was Owen Broadhurst.

"No," the lawyer said blankly. "I guess I missed it."

Andar frowned. "It landed somewhere near the colony. If we can find it, we can use it to get Laban to a doctor."

He didn't mention anything beyond that. Not yet.

Broadhurst nodded. "Of course."

"Ciejek," said Mara, "it's your turn. You and the lawyer."

Andar looked back at Mara and Emphalelo, who had been carrying Laban on her stretcher. They looked like they were about to drop from heat exhaustion.

"No problem," said Andar.

He and Broadhurst took the stretcher from the others and trudged on through the scrub grass toward the colony. The sun had already begun its descent.

Soon it would be dark.

Bet-Karh had studied the vessel as it dropped across the sky. Even at maximum magnification, it had been little more than a dark smudge against a darkening slate, but now it was becoming larger and more distinct.

He could see that it had markings on its flanks, as well as a brightly colored symbol of some sort underneath. Its descent looked to match the estimates from the Hish ship, so the hunters would meet the craft as it landed as long as they kept up their current ground-eating pace.

By then, the colony too had become visible to the hunters, if only in silhouette. The domes Bet-Karh saw were different from the architecture he was used to, but his Hunts had taken him to other exotic locales. This was just another variation on an old theme, another new hunting environment among many others.

Heith-Rek suggested, between harsh, clicking breaths, that they just shoot the ship down and be done with it. His clan-mate thought it was a good idea as well, and said so. However, Bet-Karh wouldn't countenance such a thing.

The Hunt, he reminded his comrades, was a sacred tradition. It was not to be dirtied for the sake of convenience. It was to be drawn out and savored, as their forebears decreed, not demeaned by talk of slaughter from afar.

Heith-Rek looked to be formulating a response when they heard a roar overhead, reminding them that the craft was approaching the ground, and quickly.

With hand gestures, Bet-Karh directed his fellow hunters to flank him on either side. This way, they would already be in position when the craft opened its doors. At the same time, they activated their personal cloaking devices, so they could choose the time and the manner in which they confronted their prey.

The small ship kicked up a fair amount of dirt as it stopped short of the ground and hovered for a moment above a small, black landing pad. The markings on the pad made no sense to Bet-Karh, but they no doubt held some meaning for the humans. Slowly, as if its occupants were in no particular hurry, the craft touched down.

Had they known they were in the presence of Hish, Bet-Karh thought, they might not have landed at all. But as far as they could tell, they were alone in the night, and there was no reason to be wary.

Bet-Karh checked the readouts on his helmet display and made certain his plasma weapon was charged. His plan was to let the humans disembark and close the door of their craft behind them. Then he would take one of them down as a signal that the Hunt was on. At that point, he would allow the humans to run before he picked out a single target and began tracking him.

Nearly two minutes passed before a rear door slid open and a man, weapon in hand, emerged from the craft. He looked left and then right, surveying the landscape, before he gestured for his comrades to follow. One by one, they disembarked.

Heith-Rek looked eager to begin killing then and there. However, it was up to the leader to take the first victim, and Bet-Karh hadn't made a move yet. So like it or not, Heith-Rek would have to wait.

Bet-Karh counted ten humans in all, all save one of the same gender. Each of them appeared armed with a variety of weapons, which might make them a bit more difficult to bring down. Bet-Karh hoped so. *The more challenging the prey*, he thought, *the worthier the Hunt*.

With the humans assembled outside the craft, the vehicle's door slid closed again. Bet-Karh felt Heith-Rek's scrutiny, but ignored it. He would begin the Hunt when he was ready, and not a moment before.

One of the humans, their leader apparently, pointed toward the domes of the colony. The others made speech-sounds, which were indecipherable to Bet-Karh. He could mimic them if he wished, but their meaning was lost on him.

Raising his helmet a touch, the hunter targeted the human closest to him. All three red targeting-laser points found the man's upper spine. But Bet-Karh wouldn't shoot his prey in the back, as his clan considered such a shot cowardly. Instead, he lowered the aiming mechanism on his weapon and targeted the human's feet.

Slowly, Bet-Karh squeezed off a shot—and the human's boots nearly exploded. Screaming in pain, he toppled over. Instantly, the other humans scattered, hitting the ground or running. None attempted to return to the ship or to offer assistance to his fallen comrade.

Some of the humans seemed eager to return Bet-Karh's fire, but they didn't know where the attack had come from. Nor would they until he chose to de-cloak.

Meanwhile, the wounded man writhed in agony, trying with his hands to beat out the flames that engulfed his pants. Bet-Karh walked past him, ignoring him. The human would likely perish from loss of blood before he could become a threat again—but not so quickly that he wouldn't be available for interrogation.

After all, the Hish still had to find out how they had been lured here. Without that information, the Hunt would not be complete.

As Bet-Karh selected a target, so did Heith-Rek and Mor-Jut. Bet-Karh didn't expect to see either one of them until after the Hunt was over. And that was as it should be. The best Hunt was one in which the hunter hunted alone.

Bet-Karh watched his chosen prey run between two domed buildings. Rather than pursue him directly, the hunter decided to take a different route and cut him off. As the human would find out, the Hish could be fleet of foot when they wanted to be.

With the last of the sun's light ebbing away, Bet-Karh manipulated the sights on his helmet to allow him to see in infrared. He had hunted so often in the dark, he had grown more comfortable with infrared than with anything else.

As he ran, he made a decision to eschew the use of his plasma caster. He had always found his knives to be a more satisfying option. In an open field, they weren't especially practical—

but in these close quarters, they were clearly the weapon of choice.

Tensing a muscle in his arm, he released the blades. They sprang out with a pronounced *slikt* and remained there, long and sharp and eminently lethal.

As Bet-Karh made his way among the domes, he registered shouts and gunfire and the scrape of boot soles on gravel. Each Hunt had its own rhythm, its own pattern of sounds. Judging by what he was hearing, his comrades' hunts were going well.

Another few seconds, Bet-Karh judged, and he would converge with his prey. He could hear the pelting of the human's footfalls, getting closer and closer. He lifted his bladed wrist in eager anticipation . . . .

Bet-Karh believed he had timed his appearance perfectly, but the human was nowhere in sight. Listening carefully, the hunter heard his target's footfalls again, but they were retreating. Had his prey heard his approach?

Running harder, Bet-Karh came around the curved surface of the dome and saw the human. He was running away as fast as his legs could carry him. He glanced back over his shoulder—a sure sign that he was aware of his pursuer, cloak or no cloak.

For the sake of sport, Bet-Karh dropped the cloak. The sight of him elicited a cry of surprise from the human, who stumbled and almost fell as a result of the distraction.

Bet-Karh wished he could smell his prey's fear. Unfortunately, his helmet prevented that. And if he removed it, he would have no infrared vision with which to hunt.

Suddenly, Bet-Karh heard a crack. In almost the same moment, he felt the impact of a bullet against his left arm. His armor, however, was more than capable of deflecting a single, lucky shot.

Without breaking stride, he continued his pursuit. More bullets came his way, but they went astray. The shooter was clearly unnerved by the prospect of what would happen when Bet-Karh caught up to him.

Two more bullets struck the hunter in rapid succession, both in the leg. But the armor plating there kept them from doing any damage. Bet-Karh kept going, undaunted.

Then the human *did* fall, so intent on the hunter that he had failed to notice something in his way. He sprawled, rolled, and came up hard against the base of a dome. And in the process, he lost his firearm.

With a few more strides, Bet-Karh brought himself within striking distance. The human struggled to his feet and tried to save himself, but it was too late. The hunter's arm shot forward, piercing soft skin and internal organs alike.

The human's scream was little more than a choked cry. His eyes rolling back in his head, he left a bright red trail on the pale surface as he slid to the ground. Placing his boot heel on the body, Bet-Karh dragged his knives out. With a sucking sound, they came free.

Knowing there were other targets to be acquired, he made quick work of the body. The clothes were sliced away in seconds. A twist of the wrist and he heard the spine snap. Another few swipes with his blade and the body was reduced to a bloody mess.

With his left hand, he reached in and yanked, drawing out the skull and spinal cord all at once. His right hand deftly and expertly cut away the bits of rib and clinging organs, as blood pooled by his feet. Of course, he would have to wait to treat the trophy.

Tucking the bony spinal cord under his belt, he allowed the skull to fall against his hip. Then he whipped about in search of his next victim. Judging by the cries he heard, there was a Hunt in progress not too far away—just around the next dome, in fact.

But rather than circumvent the intervening dome, he decided to try another approach. Cloaking himself again, he dug his clawed hands into the taut but yielding material of the dome and pulled himself up the side of it. Then he dragged out his claws and dug them in again, higher up. And in that manner, he made his way to the top of the rounded structure.

Crouching there, he looked down at the human pathways around him. He could see neither Hish nor prey—at least at first. But after a moment or two, a pair of humans rushed into sight, their heat signatures pulsing a bright red. They were looking back over their shoulders as they fled, firing energy beams at something they couldn't see.

But Bet-Karh, with his infrared vision, could see the hunter pursuing them. Mor-Jut's signature was different from that of the humans—larger, more intense. Bet-Karh paused to watch the chase, appreciating it as much for what it was as for how it would end.

The humans were keeping up an impressive pace, refusing to be trapped. It was a good Hunt. From his vantage point, Bet-Karh could have ended it with two well-placed blasts of his plasma caster. However, he didn't want to spoil the Hunt. Certainly, he would have been angry if one of the other hunters had done such a thing to *him*.

Instead, he found a new target—an unexpected one, as a human crested one of the domed surfaces less than a hundred feet away. Bet-Karh found it entertaining that this human thought as he did. But then, taking the high ground was one of the first principals of armed encounters.

Unlike Bet-Karh, however, the human was unaware that there was anyone else up there. Such was the value of the personal cloak. It gave the Hish an almost unworthy advantage.

Calculating the distance from dome to dome, the hunter took a deep breath, coiled, and sprang. Sailing through the air, he came down halfway up the curved wall of the next dome, and used his claws to anchor himself there.

He could see his prey, a brilliant crimson in his field of vision. The human was looking in Bet-Karh's direction, though he couldn't see anything there, his weapon at the ready.

This is too easy, the hunter told himself.

He decided to drop his cloak again, this time for good. He also determined that he would avoid not only the plasma caster, but his knives as well. In that way, his prey might prove more of a challenge.

When the human caught sight of Bet-Karh, he scrabbled backward in panic and blurted, "Oh shit!"

Intrigued by the sound, Bet-Karh repeated it: "Oh shit!"

It was then that the human seemed to remember he had a weapon in his hand. Leveling it at the hunter, he squeezed off an energy beam. But Bet-Karh ducked, and the beam dealt him only a glancing blow.

A second time, the human fired. And a second time the hunter eluded the brunt of the attack. Then it was Bet-Karh's turn.

Rushing forward up the curve of the dome, he grabbed the human by his shirtfront and lifted him off his perch with one hand. The human kicked at him, striking him in the face. But the impact wasn't enough to make Bet-Karh let go.

Instead, he struck the human back.

The sound of breaking bones surprised him. He had imagined humans to be less brittle. Still, Bet-Karh's prey remained feisty, swinging a fist at the hunter's chest.

The impact was lighter than before, hardly an impact at all from the hunter's point of view. But out of desperation and fear, the human kept hitting him. After a little while, the human's breathing got wet and ragged, and the blows began to miss Bet-Karh altogether.

"Oh, shit!" he said, mocking his victim's expression.

Then, bored with the encounter, Bet-Karh lifted up his adversary and slammed him down across his bent, armored knee. With a crack, the human's spine shattered. But he was still alive, twitching.

Not that it made any difference to Bet-Karh. As before, he extended his knife and set to work extracting his trophy.

When he was done, he had two skulls and two spines under his belt, though one spine was truncated because of the way he had snapped it. While he had earned the prizes, he still felt unsatisfied. The humans hadn't been as challenging as he had hoped.

Looking down again, he surveyed the colony. To his right, he saw Heith-Rek tracking a human female. But there was another human behind Heith-Rek, appearing to hunt him in turn.

It occurred to Bet-Karh to warn Heith-Rek about the second human's presence. However, one did not offer advice to a hunter in the midst of a Hunt. To do so would have been disrespectful in the extreme. Besides, Heith-Rek was more than likely aware of the second human. What he did with his prey was his own business.

Still, Bet-Karh had to admit that he was captivated by the scenario. Hunkering down, he watched it unfold.

Heith-Rek, it seemed, had come to the same conclusion as Bet-Karh and had deactivated his plasma caster in favor of a more primitive weapon—his staff. He was ready to hurl it forward when the human behind him fired. But it wasn't a projectile or an energy beam that hit Heith-Rek. It was something red and fiery.

And it didn't just spoil Heith-Rek's aim. It went right through him, armor and all, spraying bright green blood on the ground. To Heith-Rek's credit, he didn't go down—at least not right away. But when the human saw he had wounded the hunter, he pressed his attack.

Rushing forward, he fired a second time, this time at closer range. The hunter was nearly cut in two by the ensuing blast.

As he collapsed face forward, Bet-Karh attempted to mourn him for a moment, if only out of respect for Heith-Rek's clan.

But he could not bring himself to care. Heith-Rek had been a thorn in Bet-Karh's side. He would not be missed.

Instead, Bet-Karh focused on the human, who did not linger to take a trophy in the manner of the Hish. Quite the contrary. He ran away, losing himself among the domes.

Heith-Rek's demise left only two hunters—Bet-Karh and Mor-Jut—to continue the Hunt. But soon there would be more hunters arriving, and they would more than make up for the loss of Heith-Rek.

FOURTEEN

No sooner had Derek's men cleared the shuttle than something fired at them. When Sanderson's feet practically exploded, it was more than enough warning for everyone else to seek shelter.

Derek ignored the direction everyone else took and made a straight line for the dome directly before him, the largest of three. Marked as the administrative office for the landing area, it looked closed—the same as it had looked when he arrived the day before for the feast.

Not that he cared if it was *ever* open. All that he wanted from it at the moment was a place to hide himself from his enemies.

Especially since they weren't just *any* enemies—they were the damned Predators. Who else could have attacked without being seen? And who else could have beaten them to the landing site?

Putting his shoulder down, he crashed through the doorway of the dome. Then he sought a basement or maintenance tunnel, anything that would get him away from the Predators.

For a moment, he thought about what would happen to Sanderson—but it was only for a moment. Then his finely honed instinct for self-preservation took over. He had to get away from these monsters and regroup.

Only then would he be able to destroy Andar and make himself the sole Ciejek in the family business.

Grigori Wachman wasn't at all sure about what had happened. He had seen his friend Sanderson go down, screaming in pain and clutching at his ankles, having been hit by an unseen assailant.

Had their positions been reversed, Wachman was sure Sanderson would have taken off. That was why Wachman didn't feel the least bit guilty about abandoning his friend and trying to save himself.

As he ran, Wachman reached into his shoulder holster and withdrew a fat, jet-black pistol with a short, wide barrel. But he didn't fire it, because he couldn't find anyone to fire at.

The Predators could move around without being seen, or so Derek Ciejek had said. And Derek had warned them about the Predators. But until Wachman had seen that blast come out of nowhere, the deadliness of the aliens hadn't sunk in.

Unfortunately, he wasn't the fleetest of Derek's men. And Wachman knew all too well the joke about the hunters pursued by a bear. *"We're never going to outrun this bear,"* says the first one. *"I don't have to outrun the bear,"* says the other. *"I just have to outrun you."*

All the others would outrun Wachman, if it came to that. So he couldn't let it be a race.

I've got to find a place to hide, he told himself.

No sooner had the thought occurred to him than a set of doors presented themselves on his right. They gave access to a big dome, one of the biggest Wachman had seen in the colony. But he didn't want the Predators to know where he had gone, so he didn't try to force his way in. He planted his back against the doors and waited for the entrance mechanism to register his presence.

For a moment, nothing happened. *Come on*, he thought. *Open, damn it.*

As if in compliance with his unspoken command, the doors swung in and admitted him to the interior of the dome. He found himself in a dark honeycomb of an office, each work area partitioned from the next by brightly colored, freestanding walls.

As far as he could tell, the building was empty. Not that he cared. The last thing he was going to do was call out when there might be a Predator standing in the street outside.

Just as he thought that, he heard a scream for help. And another.

They caught in his gut like fishhooks. The men with whom he had descended in the shuttle had been his comrades for years. Together, they had paid their dues, kissed Derek Ciejek's ass, and spilled enough blood to fill an Olympic pool.

But they were not his family. In a fight like this, it was every man for himself, no matter what had gone before.

Wachman moved deeper into the dome, and the screams faded. He could be safe in here. The Predators didn't know who was coming down in the shuttle, did they? They could easily overlook him.

Then later, when they were gone, he could come out. *And do what?* he asked himself. *Go up into the mountains? Hide until they leave?*

It was Derek who had lured the aliens there, and let them loose on his cousin's party. *What the devil was he thinking?*

Suddenly, he heard a door slam shut behind him. Someone else was in the building. *One of the Predators?*

Sweat broke out on Wachman's forehead, and his heart began to beat faster. *This isn't the first fight you've been in*, he reminded himself. *And it won't be the last.*

To put the matter in perspective, he reviewed his ordnance. In his hand was his pistol with its eight shots. Behind his back, in a leather sheath, was a bowie knife. Strapped to his right thigh was a second knife, and on the other thigh he had another pistol.

He also had a half-dozen flash grenades hanging off his belt, designed to distract and confuse potential enemies. That would be enough for him to overcome any human adversary, but these Predators looked bigger and nastier than anything he had ever seen.

I'd sell my left arm for a bazooka, he thought.

But that wasn't an option. He would just have to make due with what he had.

His best bet, he decided, was to hunker down and try to remain quiet. That way, the Predator—if it *was* a Predator—might give up and go away. As Wachman knelt there, he scanned his surroundings.

Desks. Computers. Knickknacks and little signs intended to humanize the prefab feel of the place. He read a joke and was tempted to laugh at it, but the laugh died in his throat when he felt a presence.

Wheeling, he trained his pistol on . . . nothing.

There was no one there. But Wachman remained certain that he was not alone. The fact that he couldn't hear anything didn't lull him into a sense of security. He was certain that whoever had opened the door was still in the vicinity.

But as the minutes passed, there was still no evidence that he had company. Moving deeper into the office, he continued to glance over his shoulder. The last thing he wanted was for a Predator to surprise him by appearing behind his back.

Wachman was so intent on what was behind him, he bumped into something ahead of him. Turning to see what it was, he found himself face to face with a heavily armored giant.

The bastard had to be seven feet tall if he was an inch. On his right shoulder stood the mounted—and very deadly—plasma emitter that Derek had warned them about. Bits and pieces of skeleton dangled from the alien's armor like trophies from its previous hunts.

Swallowing back his fear, Wachman pointed his gun at the Predator's face—or whatever lurked behind its helmet—and squeezed the trigger. But the alien was too quick for him, knocking the gun aside and spoiling his aim.

Then Wachman saw the long, twin blades extend from the Predator's right wrist. Before the human could run, the alien lunged forward—and buried its blades in Wachman's gut.

The blades felt like icicles, freezing his insides, inducing a cascade of bright red blood. With a twist of its wrist, the Predator increased the damage. Wachman tried to scream, but couldn't because of the blood that was filling his mouth. The scream came out as a gurgle, nothing more.

Somehow he found the strength to reach across his belly and try to hold his organs in, while squeezing the trigger on the weapon in his other hand. The pistol went off with a sound like thunder, again and again and again. He emptied the entire clip.

The Predator laughed.

Or it sounded like a laugh, echoed through the helmet's amplification system. After all, not a single projectile had hit its target.

Cursing himself, Wachman saw his world go dim. He felt as if he were being buried in a landslide of ice. It robbed him of all feeling, all desire.

But it didn't kill him. Not yet.

He was still conscious when the Predator bent its knee and began carving the flesh from Wachman's face.

"Noooo . . . !" he screamed, but again his horror was drowned in his own blood.

The Predator didn't so much as pause in his work. He just kept on cutting.

Rene Turgeon looked to be about as wide as he was tall. His face was covered with a bushy brown beard. A black patch covered his left eye—the one he had lost in a bar fight a decade and a half earlier.

But his aim was still pretty good—good enough to have taken down one of the Predators. Not that Turgeon's light-weight, portable flamethrower was the kind of ordnance that required pinpoint accuracy. All he had to do was point it in the general direction of his adversary and the weapon's fiery barrage did the rest.

Turgeon hadn't lingered over his victory, but it still pulsed within him like a living thing. The boss had been so damned worried about the aliens. Scared, one might say. But under the right circumstances, the Predators died the same as anyone else.

And Turgeon intended to create the right circumstances as often as possible.

He had spent most of his life as a glorified leg-breaker, the last ten years in the employ of Derek Ciejek. His job was to chase down deadbeats and unwilling "associates" for Derek's various illicit ventures. It wasn't paradise but it paid the rent.

His colleagues liked running around and getting falling-down drunk when they got the chance, but Turgeon was more of a homebody. Whenever he was away, he looked forward to returning to his nice condo with its plush furniture and its custom-made bed. It made for a pleasant oasis away from the pressure of work.

Sometimes he got to share the place with a "guest"—one of the wretched souls who had sold themselves into inden-tured servitude rather than starve on a declining outworld.

Derek was good at purchasing the services of such people for a pittance. Most of them were used in factories, high-risk shipping ventures, or occasionally the homes of the wealthy. Some were made available to Derek's most-valued muscle.

Usually, Turgeon selected a woman. These he pampered—at least at first. He would delight in getting to know them, making them feel safe and wanted. They would be fed, given soft, expensive things to wear, and spared from doing household chores.

This would go on for a few days, work permitting. Then he would show them a different side of his nature. They would become his personal playthings, indulging him in any activity that tickled his fancy, no matter how bizarre.

Some of the women responded positively to Turgeon's attentions. But not many. Most of them fought him until he beat them into submission—an unfortunate consequence, but a necessary one.

No matter who they were, he eventually grew bored with them. At that point he returned them to his boss for "recycling" and selected someone else. A good deal all around.

Occasionally, Turgeon selected a man from Derek's inventory. But not for sex. He took the men to an apartment he maintained, not as nice as his own but a reasonably comfortable one. He saw to it that they were fed and clothed and generally in good health.

Then he activated a program he had developed that would select a random point in the wilderness outside the compound. The following morning, Turgeon would hire an aircraft and have the man brought to that spot. Once he left the plane, the man was given some basic camping supplies, appropriate clothing for the climate, and a twelve-hour head start.

At the end of the twelve hours, Turgeon would hunt the man down. If the fellow eluded him for the next twenty-four hours, Turgeon would give him a card accessing a modest bank account and the man would be given his freedom. If Turgeon tracked the man successfully, he would kill him.

A reasonable deal, he mused.

So in a way, he was more like a Predator than he was like his fellow humans. He liked hunting people down. And he was good at it—as evidenced by the alien he had burned to a crisp.

Senses alert, Turgeon made his way around a dome, seeking a sign of one of the other aliens. In the process, he caught sight of an unusual structure—a half-dome with large bay doors, which had been left open. As he got closer, he saw that the floor had various ramps, tracks, and pits in it, the kind one might find in a maintenance-and-repair facility.

Given its proximity to the landing pad, he imagined this place was for small craft. Shuttles, primarily. He wondered if there was anything in there that he might use as a weapon against the aliens.

Taking a few steps inside, he peered into the gloom at the back of the facility. Unable to see anything, he went deeper. And deeper still. Finally, he caught sight of something. Against the wall to his right were several bright red tanks with digital meters atop each one. Short hoses led from the tanks to an igniter, indicating they were welding devices.

Unfortunately, he couldn't do anything with them— unless he wanted to carry them around on his back. And he already had a flamethrower cradled in his arms, so what was the point?

He had barely finished asking himself the question when he heard the whir of something mechanical. Turning, he saw the facility's bay doors sliding closed. There was no way for him to stop them, either. As he looked on, they came together—and shut off the light from outside, plunging the maintenance facility into darkness.

Turgeon wished he could believe the doors' closing was just a coincidence. But it wasn't. One of the aliens had trapped him inside—and more than likely, trapped itself in there with him.

After all, that was what *he* would have done if he were hunting someone.

Not good, Turgeon thought, staring into the darkness. He could feel his forehead break out in sweat.

Luckily, he had some options. His left hand flexed once, twice, and a yellow tongue of burning liquid emerged from the tip of his flamethrower. Using it as a light, he started all the way to his left and arced right, scanning the interior of the dome.

The whole time, he was aware of the tanks of flammable liquid standing behind him. All the Predator had to do was fire at those tanks and the whole place would go up in a big fireball. But Turgeon didn't think the alien would do that—not when it would mean suicide.

Where are you? the human thought, trying to pick out a shape in the darkness.

Of course, that presupposed that the Predator wasn't cloaked. If Turgeon were the hunter, he wouldn't have remained invisible. That would have made it too easy.

Come on, he thought, *give me a break here.*

His flame lit up a space maybe a dozen feet in diameter. He sensed the shapes of things around him and stepped carefully so as not to trip on a track or a pit cover. He also listened for his adversary, but the soft hiss from his flamethrower masked external noises.

Nothing.

Turgeon felt his heart start to beat a little harder. He didn't mind a hunt, but he hated waiting games.

Increasing the flow of fuel, he lengthened his flame. The downside of that was that he would run out of fuel faster, but at that point he had little choice in the matter. He had to find the alien.

Don't be a pussy, he thought. *Show yourself.*

Turgeon jabbed his flame in one direction and then another, hoping for a lucky hit. He charged here and there at random. He even taunted the alien, knowing all the while it probably didn't understand a word he said.

What he *never* did, not even once, was look up.

So when the Predator leapt from its perch on a shelf above, landing beside Turgeon, the human was caught entirely off-guard. The alien's blow sent him stumbling backward.

Recovering, Turgeon trained his flame on his attacker and turned up the intensity. But by then, the Predator had cloaked itself again, and was nowhere to be seen.

Turgeon got an idea. Turning about in a full circle, he let his flame's heat fill the air. He then looked very carefully for any ripple that would give away the alien's presence.

He was still looking when he felt a blow from behind, a savage kick that sent him pitching forward. He nearly burned his face as he fell, managing to avoid his flame by mere inches.

As he scrambled back to his feet, he heard the unmistakable sound of metal against metal. Apparently, the alien was arming itself with something other than its plasma gun. *Good.*

As before, he poked the air with his flame. Before he knew it, his arm was caught in a grip like steel and twisted sharply, forcing him to drop the flamethrower. But now he knew where the Predator was.

His fist, which was sheathed in a brass knuckle-like device, shot out and connected with something soft and yielding—right where Turgeon figured the alien's throat would be. It was a lucky shot but an effective one. Turgeon felt the pressure on his arm go away.

Building on his advantage, Turgeon swung at his invisible adversary a second time, and a third. But all he hit was armor. Then an unseen blow to the jaw sent him hurtling backward, lights flashing behind his eyes.

He might have blacked out were it not for the burning pain in his hand, which had been caught by the fringe of his flame. Screaming in agony, he tucked the hand into his belly and groped for the flamethrower, knowing it was his only chance.

Come to Papa, Turgeon thought. *Please . . .*

Suddenly, his fingers found what they were looking for and wrapped themselves around the barrel of the flamethrower. He had a chance. He could still win this thing and come out alive.

Then, in the pale light thrown by his weapon, Turgeon saw a trio of red dots appear on the flamethrower's barrel. For a moment, he didn't know what they were. Then he remembered what the boss had said about them . . .

And had a sinking feeling he knew what would come next.

Coming out of nowhere, the single white bolt struck the flamethrower in its fuel supply, igniting it. A curse formed in Turgeon's mouth, a desperate and colorful curse, the kind he was known for back at the Ciejeks' compound.

But the explosion tore him apart before he could utter it.

All she wanted was one lousy cigarette.

Liz Myers couldn't imagine enduring hours, if not days, in the underground shelters without her beloved drug of choice. Sure, she knew cigarettes caused cancer and could kill her. She also knew she drank too much, and no doubt was doing damage to her brain and internal organs.

Still, she had come to Felicity to escape the horrors of Earth and start anew. She had dyed her hair blonde, seen to it she never again topped 110 pounds, and taken injections to make her lips full and pouty. Smoking and drinking were her only vices, counteracted by vigorous exercise and an unwavering devotion to Felicity's mining industry.

She didn't know why the alarm had been sounded or why everybody had been herded into the reinforced-dome shelters on the south side of the colony. However, she did know that the shelters were to be locked exactly thirty minutes after the alarm sounded.

That was maybe twenty-five minutes ago. Plenty of time for that last invigorating cigarette, she had insisted. The security guard overseeing her assigned shelter had seen it otherwise.

To underline the urgency of her plight, Liz had stuck her tongue in his ear and whispered there was more where that came from. Seeing her request in a new light, the security officer authorized her to stand outside for a few minutes—no longer.

So there she was, standing outside, taking deep, long drags of her cigarette. Trying not to let a single molecule of nicotine go to waste.

She was a few drags from the end when she heard an explosion, a scream, and a strange, sickly, sucking sound. It was awfully nearby, though she couldn't see the cause of it, and it made all the hair on her arms and neck stand on end. Deciding to practice some discretion, she stubbed out the last quarter-inch of the cigarette and knocked on the door to be let back in.

As she waited for a response, she saw something red drip in front of her from above. Craning her neck to look up, she saw something looking down at her from the domed roof. It was gigantic, with a skull-like metal mask over its face and some kind of braids falling over one massive, armored shoulder.

Liz wanted to scream but couldn't seem to engage her vocal chords.

With amazing agility, the armored monstrosity leaped from the top of the building and landed at her feet. Slowly, it straightened to its full height. It was even bigger than she had thought.

Her knees shook, too weak for her to run on them. She threw her cigarette at the monster, a useless gesture. She stood helpless, in silent terror.

As she stared, mesmerized, the giant reached out and grabbed her by the throat. Suddenly, Liz Myers could no longer breathe, let alone scream. As the giant's fingers closed around her windpipe and she began to black out, she knew she was going to die.

Her last thought, as her neck cartilage began to snap, was how fine that last cigarette had tasted.

Derek crouched in the lee of a dome and looked around. He had left his previous safe hiding place, unable to stand the silence.

It was clear to him that an alarm had gone off at some point, and that people had fled from their homes and businesses. Otherwise, the streets in this part of the colony wouldn't have been so eerily empty.

Derek's shuttle hadn't been greeted by the Predators more than fifteen minutes earlier, and yet the colony had already taken shelter. *Impressive*, he thought. Even his family compound wouldn't have been able to respond so quickly.

Marlene, who was hunkered down behind him, put a hand on his back. "Where the hell is everyone?" she breathed.

"How the hell should I know?" he shot back.

Marlene had caught up with him after he escaped the firefight. He wasn't surprised. She had a knack for survival, just as he did. That was one of the things he had always liked about her.

In order to keep on surviving, they had to find shelter. It wouldn't do to be the only ones out on the streets when the Predators started prowling around. As if to add emphasis to the thought, a scream came from the direction of the landing field.

Frowning, Derek grabbed Marlene by the arm and pulled her in the opposite direction. If they found a shelter, they could demand admittance. After all, he was Derek Ciejek. His family owned this place.

Yeah, he thought, *that's the ticket*.

They just had to find a shelter.

FIFTEEN

Andar and his party had made it over the mountains and were within spitting distance of the colony when they caught sight of the shuttle again. It was on the ground less than a mile away, a low, sleek shadow looking lonely in the gathering dark.

"Just a little longer," he whispered to Laban, whose features were scrunched up in pain despite the injection they had given her.

But then, it wasn't very strong—just what they could find in the med kit. And they had used up the last of it. When it wore off, Laban would be forced to bear the pain in full.

All the more reason to get her to a doctor, Andar reflected.

His hands were sore and cramped from carrying his end of the stretcher for so long, but he was encouraged by the sight of the shuttle. Unless he missed his guess, they would reach it in a matter of minutes. Then they could get Laban the help she needed.

He was feeling good about that until he heard the crack of gunfire—not once, but twice. He looked at Mara, then Emphalelo, and finally at Broadhurst.

"The Predators," he said, voicing what all of them were thinking.

"They must have taken a different route," said Mara, the muscles in his jaw fluttering.

Andar should have known that finding a physician for Laban wouldn't be so easy. For all he knew, the aliens were still in the vicinity, looking for prey. Or they might have moved off—it was hard to tell until they reached the shuttle.

"It's going to be okay," he whispered to Laban, undaunted by the shift in circumstances. "We'll get you out of here."

She murmured in acknowledgment.

Laban had been a pillar of strength since Gregor's death. She was the center of his operation, the engine that made it work. Andar needed her, maimed as she was. He needed her mind and her strength of character, for the sake of everyone who still worked for Andar's side of the family.

"It's going to be okay," he told her again.

This time, she didn't answer.

"Check your weapons," said Andar. "We're going in, Predators or no Predators."

Mara and Emphalelo exchanged looks and did as Andar suggested. So did Broadhurst, though he was more than a little clumsy about it. No one could afford to take chances anymore.

Not even Andar himself. Leaving one hand on the stretcher handle, he used the other to remove his pistol from his pocket and look it over. Then he put it back, leaving the pocket flap open.

They hadn't heard anything since those first two reports, but that didn't mean anything. The aliens might still be out there. But none of the humans slowed down or suggested another option. Everyone knew he had to do this—not just for Laban, but for himself.

"Who do you think was on that shuttle?" Broadhurst asked him, doing his best to manage the front of the stretcher.

"Don't know," Andar said. "Don't care."

It was the truth. All he could think about was helping Laban, and then going after Derek. Nothing else mattered.

The closer they got to the shuttle, the more Andar expected to see an indication that the Predators were still around. But he didn't see a thing. Just the shuttle, sitting there all by itself.

They were within a quarter mile when the wind shifted and Andar smelled something—a stench like burning meat. It made him want to gag. If he'd had any lunch, he probably would have lost it.

"What is that?" asked Broadhurst.

"Don't ask," said Emphalelo.

Laban had told Andar that Emphalelo was a sensitive, somebody who could analyze a person's strengths and weaknesses without ever meeting him. *Just going on the basis of second-hand evidence,* he reflected. *Like a twenty-first century profiler.*

Someone like that had to know a lot about human nature— what a man would do or not do under a given set of circumstances. Andar wondered what Emphalelo thought of *him*. Not much probably. After all, Andar was a dilettante compared to stone-cold killers like Sildar and Trynda.

But I'm still alive, Andar thought. *Maybe that counts for something in his book.*

He was trying his best to ignore the smell when he saw the bodies. They were scattered on the ground around the shuttle—three of them that he could see. They looked like they had been mutilated.

"Bastards," said Mara.

Andar didn't want to look at them, but as he got closer he couldn't help himself. In two cases they were unrecognizable, their heads ripped off and their chests torn open. But in the third case, to his surprise, he saw a face he knew.

One of Derek's men. He didn't know the man's name, but he recognized the long features and the short-cropped blond hair from the feast the night before.

"Sanderson," said Emphalelo, supplying the name.

"Looks like his feet were blown off," Mara noted, his brow furrowed with disgust.

Derek's man, Andar thought.

So his cousin *had* been involved with the shuttle, though *how* was still difficult to say. He glanced again at the two ruined corpses and wondered if one of them was Derek. *Probably not.*

Derek liked his men to do the dirty work. He was probably holed up in a room somewhere, grumbling over their deaths, calculating how it would effect his own chances of survival.

Andar certainly hoped so. Because if Derek was on Felicity, he would find him.

Coming up behind the shuttle, Andar and Broadhurst lowered Laban to the ground. Then Mara put his hand on the touch-sensitive pad that opened and closed the rear hatch door.

Andar half-expected it to be locked, which would have presented them with a problem. But it wasn't. The hatch door accommodated them by sliding up without complaint, thereby giving them access to the interior of the craft.

"Come on," said Mara, picking up the front of the stretcher. Emphalelo picked up the back of it, and together they moved Laban inside. Then, ever so gingerly, they lifted her from the stretcher and laid her on a seat in the aft of the vessel.

Andar was satisfied. They had what they needed. Now all they had to do was find a doctor, either in this colony or the next one.

Peering past Laban, he noted the control panel in the fore of the craft. From where he stood, it didn't look all that complicated—less so, in fact, than some of the craft he had flown back on Earth.

He started forward so he could check it out up close. But before he got very far, he heard a bellow for help. *Broadhurst,* he thought.

Poking his head out of the hatch, he saw the lawyer standing a few feet away from the shuttle—but couldn't see the reason for the man's cry. Broadhurst was peeking through the door of one of the smaller domes that bordered the landing pad.

Moving to join him, Andar asked him what was wrong.

"Nothing," said Broadhurst, and he stood aside so Andar could see through the transparent door into the dome.

Inside, there were cases full of silver plastic water bottles. Andar, who hadn't had anything to drink in more than a day, swallowed longingly at the sight.

"The place is locked," Broadhurst noted. Evidently, that was the reason for his outburst.

Andar sighed. "We've got energy pistols, remember?" And he took his out to point it at the door.

But before he could fire, he caught movement out of the corner of his eye. Following it, he saw a Predator on the roof of another dome, pointing his plasma weapon in the direction of the shuttle.

No! thought Andar. *For the love of God, no!*

Mara and Emphalelo had come out of the shuttle to see what Andar and Broadhurst were up to. But Laban was still laid out inside.

"Get her out!" Andar yelled across the landing area.

Mara and Emphalelo hesitated, not knowing what he was saying or why.

"Now!" Andar insisted—and he fired at the Predator on the roof.

But it was too late. The alien had vanished. And in the same breath, Andar saw the by-now familiar triangle of red dots on the side of the shuttle.

A howl of pain and sorrow emerged from him, wordless and primeval, and echoed across the landing pad. But only for a moment, because after that the Predator's plasma bolt turned the shuttle into a shuddering, screeching ball of fire.

With Laban inside.

Andar was sent flying by a hard, hot wall of concussive force. When he regained his equilibrium his ears were ringing, and he was entangled with Broadhurst.

Extricating himself, he recovered his weapon and looked to the rooftop where the Predator had disappeared. He couldn't see anything, but he fired anyway.

Again. And again. But his energy beams kept on going, uninterrupted. And nothing fired back at him. For some reason, the Predator seemed to have departed.

Andar looked back at the place where the shuttle had stood. There was nothing left of it except for a hot, smoking slag heap and melted tarmac. Fortunately, Mara and Emphalelo had survived as well, though Mara's clothes had been singed by the blast.

Andar forced himself to take stock of the situation.

Their only means of transportation—indeed, the entire colony's only means of transportation—was gone. The Predators were loose. And Laban was dead.

So why was it all he could think about was Derek?

SIXTEEN

His back pressed against a dome, Bet-Karh allowed himself to slide down its surface until he reached the ground. Then he de-cloaked and detached the breathing tubes from his helmet. Finally, he removed the helmet from his head.

The atmosphere still tasted wrong to him, but he wouldn't have to put up with it for long. Reaching into a compartment in his armor, he withdrew a protein stick, which he broke with his mandibles and consumed.

The humans were proving more elusive and ingenious than he would have believed. They were worthy prey after all for the Two Clans That Had Become One.

In fact, they had killed two of his three companions. Only Mor-Jut still lived. Bet-Karh had dispatched him to meet the newcomers and bring them to Bet-Karh—one of the privileges of being the Leader of the Hunt. And in the meantime, Bet-Karh had seen to it that the humans didn't escape.

After he destroyed their craft, he could have destroyed the four around it as well. But he refrained. He wanted to gather himself, to consider how he would treat the newcomers. There would be plenty of time for hunting humans later.

The problem, as Bet-Karh saw it, was that Heith-Rek and Kaj-Nal had entered into a debate with him every time he made a decision. Somehow, he had given them the impression that they had a voice in devising their hunting strategies. He would have to make sure the newcomers didn't labor under the same misconception.

Otherwise, the Hunt might turn into chaos, and that would bode badly for the future of their joined clan. But Bet-Karh wouldn't make the same mistake twice. He would do whatever was necessary to make sure the Hunt was a success.

He absently caressed the skull on his right hip as he thought about Heith-Rek. No doubt, Kirs-Giras would have questions about the nature of his kinsman's death, and more than questions. He would imply treachery on Bet-Karh's part, because that was his way.

It was true that Bet-Karh had done nothing to prevent Heith-Rek's destruction. However, he could not be accused of having caused it. He had simply allowed Heith-Rek to conduct his Hunt the way he wished.

As he thought that, he heard someone approaching. Replacing his helmet on his head, he consulted his visor—and picked up the approach of five figures. All were Hish.

Mor-Jut had done his job.

From a distance, only he stood out, his armor covered with a layer of dirt. But Bet-Karh could tell the others apart by subtle differences—their bearing, the way they walked, their wariness or lack of it. There was only one surprise in the bunch.

A novice, he mused, noting the shortest and most slender of the figures. They had sent him a stripling. But then, everyone had to experience First Hunt sometime, and he supposed this was as good an opportunity as any.

Bet-Karh stood to greet the newcomers in the ritual manner. The novice wasn't allowed to speak to the Leader of the Hunt without being introduced to him first. A hunter called Mal-Rek, from Kirs-Giras's clan, performed that function.

He introduced the novice as Pran-Ser, a female. Kirs-Giras had sent her because, of all the youngsters, she seemed the most capable and the most dedicated. He—Kirs-Giras—was certain that she would hunt well.

But Bet-Karh was more intent on Mal-Rek than Pran-Ser. After all, Mal-Rek was Heith-Rek's brother. Before long, he would note the absence of Heith-Rek and inquire about it.

It took even less time than Bet-Karh had imagined. No sooner had Mal-Rek completed the introduction than he asked about Heith-Rek. But his tone made it sound more like a *demand*.

Being the leader, Bet-Karh had to tell Mal-Rek the truth. But he also knew that as arrogant as Heith-Rek had been, Mal-Rek was worse. He and Mal-Rek had nearly come to blows on one occasion, immediately after the merging of their clans.

He was concerned that Mal-Rek would attack him when he found out Heith-Rek was dead. As good as Bet-Karh was with weapons, Mal-Rek was better at hand-to-hand combat.

But Mal-Rek didn't attack him when he heard the news. He said he had expected his brother to die on a Hunt. If Heith-Rek had hunted well and often in his time on this world, it was all anyone could ask.

Considering Mal-Rek's personality, Bet-Karh didn't think he would remain so accepting indefinitely. Maybe he would take his anger and sorrow out on the humans instead of Bet-Karh. And maybe not.

Mal-Rek asked after the prey. Bet-Karh explained that they had scattered, gone into hiding. But they would not be difficult to find.

Pran-Ser was eager to get started. She was excited that there was still prey for her to hunt and that a First Kill remained possible. The fact that the humans had killed two hunters didn't seem to daunt her in the least.

But then, Bet-Karh had been optimistic too, on the occasion of his First Hunt. It was not so long ago, on a world of storms and rock, where the largest life forms were lumbering, dun-colored beasts that stored and discharged pure electricity.

The Hunt took days, he remembered, as the beasts' defenses made a clean kill nearly impossible. When one was finally trapped and then killed with a long blade, Bet-Karh had savored the moment, thrusting his hands into the gaping wound and tearing the skin apart. Hot, deep-red blood had flowed over his hands and arms, staining his armor and leaving his knife-hilt permanently discolored.

He wished much the same for Pran-Ser. But first things first.

Before they embarked on this new stage of the Hunt, Bet-Karh wanted to establish his law. The six of them would have to do things according to the rules of one clan—his, since he was the leader. No other approach would be considered.

Blay-Kral growled an objection, which was echoed by his clan-brother Mal-Rek. Neither wanted his way of life ignored. Bad enough, they said, that they had to coexist with Bet-Karh's clan on the ship. There, they watched how they acted and what they said. But here? No one would tell them how to *hunt*.

Bet-Karh had expected their resistance. But he didn't give in. He said this was a situation that required a singularity of mind. The humans had proven themselves resourceful, not just on this occasion but also on many others recorded by the Hish.

Blay-Kral disagreed—vehemently. Humans were just another animal to hunt down, he said.

The Way of the Hunt, Mal-Rek added, was precious and not negotiable. He reminded Bet-Karh that clans had warred over such matters. Pran-Ser moved toward Mal-Rek, silent but supportive of her clan-mate.

But Bet-Karh had his supporters as well. One was Wrak-Oto, a female. She took a position on Bet-Karh's right flank, matching Mor-Jut's position on the leader's left. The clans need to cooperate in order to survive, she reminded them, and they needed this Hunt to be a model of that cooperation.

But Mal-Rek was having none of it. He would be damned, he said, if he would go on a Hunt without following the ways

of his father's fathers. He suggested that they split into two
Hunting parties. One would follow him while the other
followed Bet-Karh—making circles around their prey until
they were too old to hunt.

After all, he added, that is their way.

Mor-Jut had heard enough. With rapid clicks of his mandibles and a low growl, he extended his blades and rushed
forward, ready to rip Mal-Rek's flesh from his bones.

Just in time, Bet-Karh wrapped his arms around Mor-Jut
and swung him away from his target. The contemptuous Mal-
Rek, meanwhile, had extended his own blades and was rearing
back to strike when he saw whom he would be stabbing—not
Mor-Jut, but Bet-Karh, the individual charged by both Kirs-
Garas and Dre-Nath to lead the Hunt.

He didn't hold back his strike, either because he couldn't or
he didn't wish to. Fortunately, as Mal-Rek's blades sliced the
air, Bet-Karh was able to hang on to Mor-Jut a fraction of a
second longer—so that his momentum carried him away from
the offending blades.

As it was, they grazed his armor. But they did not draw
blood—a sinful act that neither clan would have condoned.
Mal-Rek, still seething, still had the upper hand, his blades
extended, his adversaries off-balance. And though he hadn't
struck yet, he was still in a position to do so.

Bet-Karh glared at Mal-Rek, asserting his authority. And
yet Mal-Rek didn't stand down. For several long moments, he
looked as if he would sink his blades into Bet-Karh's chest.

Finally Mal-Rek withdrew his blades, and with a sound of
disgust turned his back on Bet-Karh. It was a sign that he
intended no bloodshed. But it was also a sign of disrespect,
considering the status conferred upon Bet-Karh.

The leader could not let the moment pass without addressing
the other hunter's insolence. Without hesitation, he announced
that they would move the Hunt to the far side of the settle-

ment, where the prey was—and that Mal-Rek was to bring up the rear in their line of march.

Everyone looked at Mal-Rek to see his reaction.

He obviously resented the announcement, but he didn't balk. Maybe, in the privacy of his own mind, he acknowledged that Bet-Karh was right. In any case, he waited until the others had gone by and only then fell into line.

Satisfied, at least for now, Bet-Karh looked forward to the next stage of the Hunt.

SEVENTEEN

Derek Ciejek reminded himself that there was strength in numbers. And he knew what kind of numbers he had on his side, since three of his employees had answered their cell phones to say they had survived the Predators' onslaught.

"Whom did you talk to?" Marlene asked as he pocketed his phone.

"Ibrahim, Kaganas, and Jurgens," he said. "Got the others' mailboxes."

"Only three," she muttered, her voice echoing softly in the warehouse dome where they had taken refuge.

He still had no clue where the shelters were. Then again, maybe it wouldn't be such a good idea to cower with the colony's sheep. Too easy for a Predator to find them and kill them en masse.

Derek eyed Marlene, feeling that her desolation was a pit into which he could fall and never climb out. He could let fear take control of him and leave him vulnerable to the Predators—it would be easy. Or he could marshal his forces, whatever was left of them, and try to get away.

Survival, of course, won out. As always.

"Three," Marlene repeated.

"Plus us," he said.

"Five, then. Good thing we'll be together." She laughed, softly at first, and then more and more shrilly, her fear escalating into hysteria.

"Stop it!" he snarled, getting in her face. "*Stop* it!"

She looked up at him, saw his anger, and stopped. But the hysteria was still there. She was just keeping it inside.

"There are only four of the Predators," Derek told her. It was true, as far as he knew. "They've got a whole colony's worth of people to keep them busy. We'll make it."

Suddenly, he heard a noise at the door to the warehouse. Ducking, he listened for the sound of the newcomer's footfalls. They were too light to belong to a Predator.

Raising his head, he caught a glimpse of Arthur Holden, who had gone to work for Derek's side of the family a couple of years earlier. Holden was short and stocky, with a permanent scowl on his face. He always looked like he was in need of a shave.

"Holden," Derek called, just loudly enough for the man to hear him. "Over here."

Holden wasn't one of the three who had answered their cells. That was good. Now he had four men to back him up instead of three.

"You didn't answer your cell," Derek told him as Holden joined them.

"I couldn't," said Holden. "There was a Predator nearby." His scowl deepened. "I've got some news. Not good, I'm afraid."

"What is it?" asked Marlene, before Derek could respond.

Holden's frown deepened. "The aliens blew up the fucking ship."

Derek felt his stomach tighten. "You sure?"

"Saw it with my own eyes," said Holden. "The only silver lining is at least one of Andar's people was inside it. Maybe two or three—I'm not sure."

"But not Andar himself?" asked Derek.

Holden shook his head from side to side. "I don't think so. I couldn't see too well. Didn't want to become a target myself, if you know what I mean."

Derek knew, all right. He was concentrating on the same thing at the moment.

"Now we have no way of getting out of here," Marlene moaned.

"Actually," said Derek, "we do." He had been looking at the computer center in the warehouse, a conglomeration of a half-dozen workstations. "The next colony over may have some shuttles. And as far as we know, there aren't any Predators over there."

"At least not yet," said Holden.

As he said it, there was a sound at the door again. This time it was Ibrahim, followed closely by Jurgens.

Derek brought them up to speed. Then he sent Marlene over to the computer center to see what she could find out. It seemed to raise her spirits a little to have something to do—not that Derek gave a shit about her spirits. But she was by far the most savvy of them when it came to computers, and therefore the most likely to turn up what they needed.

"A question," said Ibrahim. "Assuming there's a vessel waiting for us at the next colony, how are we going to get there?"

"First things first," said Derek.

"Got it," said Marlene, sounding better than she had before. "The next colony is about ten kilometers to the south of here. According to this news report, as of an hour and a half ago there were four ships on their landing pad."

"Great," said Derek, smiling for the first time in what seemed like ages. "What about getting there? Where can we find some wheels?"

"I'm on it," said Marlene, bending over her work again.

"Boss," hissed Ibrahim, and pointed to the door.

Derek listened, but didn't hear anything. Then again, Kaganas could be pretty quiet when he wanted to be.

They all took out their weapons and pointed them in the direction of the entrance. Then Derek said, "Anton? That you?"

"Damned right," came the reply. "No unwanted company over there, I trust?"

"Just you," said Jurgens, following the remark with an ugly laugh.

Kaganas looked like he had just been exercising a little. He didn't look nearly as stressed out as the others.

"So where are we?" he asked Derek.

Derek told him.

"Say, Boss," Jurgens began hesitatingly, "none of us are pilots. How do you figure we're going to drive a shuttle even if we can find one?"

Derek didn't like the question. He supposed he could locate a shelter and see if there was a pilot holed up in it, but that would take time—and worse, put him out in the open when he was trying to maintain a low profile.

"Let's get to the spaceport," he said, "and take it from there."

Jurgens glanced at the others and shrugged. "Whatever you say." But none of them seemed confident in the plan.

Truth be told, Derek wasn't either. But he couldn't let his people know that. He waited just long enough for Marlene to find some ground transportation for them. Then he led them out of the warehouse.

Or rather, he let Kaganas do the leading. With his size, his strength, and his experience, he was the best equipped for the job.

Derek had the information he needed. He knew what he had to do.

But there were too many unknowns for his liking. When he first hatched his scheme to lure the Predators to Felicity, every scenario had him watching the fun from afar. Now he was in the middle of the action, exactly where he didn't want to be.

Once out of the warehouse, they headed southwest toward a facility where ground vehicles could be hired out—or stolen.

Derek wasn't pleased to see that the streetlights had gone on, illuminating the deserted streets. That fact could only help the Predators, who could cloak themselves in light as easily as in darkness.

He wished he knew where they were and what they were doing. Did they ever sleep? Were they wreaking havoc in one of the domes, killing at will?

For all he knew, they were walking right behind him, stalking him. *No*, he thought, *that kind of thinking's going to lead to panic.* Whatever the aliens were doing, it was all right with him—as long as it didn't include shooting at Derek Ciejek.

It was less than a mile to the ground-vehicle facility, and they got there without incident. There were two small, open vehicles outside with wide treads and complex detailing, obviously designed for multiple terrains.

Derek turned to Jurgens, who was more familiar with such things than the rest of them. "Go make them purr," he instructed.

While Jurgens got to work, the others turned their backs to him and trained their weapons on the street in either direction. Even more strongly than before, Derek got the feeling that there was a Predator right behind him, its eyes boring holes in the back of his skull. With an effort, he resisted the impulse to turn and fire.

After a minute or so, Jurgens got one vehicle going. The other took even less time, as he had become familiar with the sensor technology that triggered its engine ignition.

"Nice job," said Ibrahim.

But the last word turned into an expression of surprise and agony, as the razor-thin man was lifted off his feet. As he jerked like a puppet on an invisible string, blood blossomed from a hole in his chest.

Kaganas let out a shout: "Predators!"

For a moment, Derek froze in place. Though he couldn't see it, he imagined the pike that had plunged through Ibrahim and extended out the front of the man's chest. Mesmerized, he watched Ibrahim squirm in pain, eyes bulging, unable to dislodge the intruder inside him.

Bellowing, Holden fired his gun at Ibrahim's unseen assailant. But for his trouble he received a plasma bolt in the gut. He was dead before he hit the ground, a smoking lump of blackened flesh.

Someone pulled Derek into one of the vehicles and yanked the door closed beside him. Jurgens, who was sitting in the driver's seat, cried out for everyone to hold on. Then they were rolling, describing a wide arc in order to miss Ibrahim and his invisible assailant.

Derek saw a blast of white energy sear the air in front of them, missing Jurgens's vehicle by inches. Jurgens cursed out loud, but kept driving. Before long, they had left Ibrahim and Holden—and whoever had attacked them—behind.

Derek was glad, and not just because they were out of immediate danger. Desperately, he tried to wipe the picture of Ibrahim's agony out of his mind. He had never seen anyone in so much pain.

And he had been standing next to Ibrahim, hadn't he? It could easily have been Derek impaled on that invisible pike. Swallowing, he watched Jurgens whip them around the curvature of a dome, putting more distance between them and the aliens.

"Which way?" Jurgens bellowed, striving to be heard over the sound of the engine.

Marlene consulted a handheld computer into which she had downloaded the data. Though her hands trembled, she was able to bark out the directions.

As Jurgens followed them, he asked, "Did you see Ibrahim? He looked like a fish on a—!"

"Never mind that!" Derek snapped at him. "Just keep your eyes on what's ahead of you!"

Jurgens didn't argue. He turned around and drove, keeping his feelings to himself.

"Why do I get the feeling," Kaganas asked in a surprisingly calm voice, "that we haven't seen the last of the aliens?"

"They don't know where we're going," said Marlene. "They can't follow us."

"They can," Derek said, though he wished he were wrong. "They've got a ship in orbit, remember? They know we've taken a vehicle. They can track us."

"Why would they want to?" asked Marlene. "They've got all those colonists to hunt."

"The colonists haven't put up a fight," Kaganas observed, his intense blue eyes focused on the street ahead of them. "We have. We're a challenge for them."

Marlene didn't say anything in response. For a while, no one did. Then, after they had gotten closer to the edge of town, Kaganas broke the silence.

"We'll never make it to the next colony," he said.

"Why do you say that?" Derek demanded.

Kaganas held his hand out to Marlene. She turned the hand-held over to him and he punched in a quick command. Then he handed the device to Derek.

The screen on the handheld showed him a map of the space between them and the next colony. The road was completely open. They would be easy to spot, easy to follow.

"We'll be the proverbial sitting ducks," Kaganas pointed out.

Derek couldn't help but agree. They needed someplace where they could hide, someplace they could defend if necessary. And it couldn't be too far away.

"Stop the car," he told Jurgens.

They rolled to a stop in the shadow of a dome. There could have been Predators around, moving to intercept them there. But they couldn't go any further until Derek made a decision.

He thought for a moment. Then he returned the handheld to Kaganas. "What's our best route to the mountains?"

The big man looked at him. "Those mines?"

"Yeah. They worked for Andar. Now they need to work for us, at least until we know we've thrown the aliens off our trail."

Kaganas's big thumb scrolled quickly until he found a topographical map among the files Marlene had downloaded. Picking a likely route, he gave Derek the handheld.

Derek examined it and nodded. Then he gave Jurgens instructions, and Jurgens started them moving through the colony again. Up ahead, just within the scope of their headlights, was flat, almost desert-like terrain.

But beyond it lay the mountains—and a chance for survival.

EIGHTEEN

Bet-Karh was angry.

The moment Blay-Kral had stabbed the human from behind, Bet-Karh had railed at him for it. True hunters did not attack their prey unseen. They gave their adversaries a fighting chance. And they did not kill without their leader's permission.

Blay-Kral didn't seem to care about Bet-Karh's philosophies. All that mattered to him was the fact of the kill, not the nature of it. He was like the deceased Heith-Rek in that respect.

But it wasn't just Bet-Karh's philosophies that should have kept Blay-Kral from striking. Blay-Kral's own clan traditions directed hunters to give easy kills to novices like Pran-Ser. The stripling was angry as well, unhappy about being ignored. No doubt, her kill-gland was pumping chemicals through her body, super-charging her for the Hunt.

Not that they weren't *all* drunk with gland chemicals. Had Bet-Karh removed his helmet, he was sure he could have smelled the kill-gland secretions in the air. But that was no excuse for Blay-Kral's taking the hunt into his own hands.

Bet-Karh grabbed Blay-Kral by the shoulder and brought his helmet into contact with Blay-Kral's. In clear and unmistakable terms, the leader said he would not tolerate disregard for his authority. His orders were inviolate—and Blay-Kral would do well to remember that, for the punishment for disobeying the Leader on a Hunt was extreme.

Blay-Kral regarded him for a moment. Then he backed off a step and lowered his head in abasement. Nodding in approval, Bet-Karh gestured for the other hunter to rejoin the Hunt.

But Bet-Karh didn't believe that Blay-Kral's gesture of submission was sincere. He resolved to watch the other hunter very, very closely.

Meanwhile, the humans had secured a ground vehicle and were moving away—not very quickly, it appeared, as the vehicle was not made for speed. But the Hish would have to move too, or lose their most promising prey. With a signal for the others to follow, Bet-Karh took off after the humans.

Before long, Mal-Rek caught up with the leader. As they ran, winding their way among the domes, Mal-Rek attempted to defend Blay-Kral's actions. They were in keeping, he said, with his clan's way of hunting, a way that deserved respect. Blay-Kral would have to try harder, Mal-Rek added, to accustom himself to Bet-Karh's leadership.

The words were intended to soothe but Bet-Karh refused to let them do so. The respect due him, as well as his clan, was being withheld. Mal-Rek and Blay-Kral signified trouble.

Once again, Bet-Karh wondered if the two clans would ever truly find a common ground. Each time he spoke with those on the ship, the tension seemed more and more like a tendon being stretched to the breaking point—and ready to snap.

When Bet-Karh was first exposed to the teachings of Kirs-Giras, he opened his mind to them. He imagined that there was something of value in them. Now he saw otherwise. Dre-Nath's point of view was the *only* one worthy of the Hish.

Up ahead, the humans' vehicle was still in sight, but it was increasing the gap between hunter and hunted. With an effort, Bet-Karh picked up the pace. He didn't wish to merely slaughter the prey, but he also did not wish to lose them.

Moving up to the front of the pack, Wrak-Oto asked Bet-Karh where the humans might be headed. Bet-Karh had no answer for his clan-mate.

While preparing for the mission, he had concentrated his studies on the forest and the colony, but little else. He hadn't expected to need any further knowledge. He saw now that it had been an oversight—one he was determined never to make again.

Suddenly, the vehicle—which had yet to clear the colony—slowed to a stop. Mor-Jut turned to Bet-Karh, seeking his insight. He had none to give. He was as surprised as his clan-brother.

Had there been a malfunction? Cloaked as they were, it would not be difficult to find out. As he approached the humans, Bet-Karh slowed down, reluctant to let his footfalls give away his proximity.

Blay-Kral and Mal-Rek, however, seemed to have other ideas. Rushing up to the fore of the hunting party, they positioned themselves for plasma fire. Before they could target the vehicle, Bet-Karh held his arm out in front of them.

A still target, with no ability to fight back, was not a worthy target. He reminded them of that fact.

Blay-Kral, still in thrall to his kill-gland, did not appear to value Bet-Karh's input on the subject. Mal-Rek, on the other hand, yielded to it and pulled Blay-Kral back. Pran-Ser's posture signified her disappointment, but Bet-Karh reassured her that her time would come. She just needed to be patient.

As they communicated, quietly so their presence wouldn't be detected, the humans' vehicle started moving again. Therefore, so did the Hish.

In moments, they came to the limits of the colony. The humans' vehicle kept going, heading out into the vast unremarkable terrain. But beyond it, in the distance . . .

The mountains, Bet-Karh reflected. The *mines*.

Some of the other humans had eluded them there. Now Bet-Karh and his party had a chance for redemption. That was good for all concerned, regardless of which clan they came from.

But first, they would have to keep the humans in sight. Though the vehicle wasn't especially fast, a long trip wouldn't tire it out. The Hunters, on the other hand, had their limits.

That wasn't a problem, from Bet-Karh's point of view. It would only make the Hunt more of a challenge.

Looking forward to it, he struck out across the flat terrain. The others followed, not one of them complaining. This was, after all, what they were born for. Regardless of clan affiliation, a hunter had to appreciate it.

They hadn't gone far when Mor-Jut reminded him it was time to check in with the ship. Using the controls in his helmet, Bet-Karh sent a signal to Dre-Nath.

But he didn't receive a response.

He looked up at the night sky and its tattered, gray clouds. As far as he knew, there was nothing in the air that would interfere with communications. Certainly, nothing had changed since his last conversation with Dre-Nath.

This disturbed him. However, his exchange with Dre-Nath could wait. They were in the midst of a Hunt—Dre-Nath would understand.

As the hunters ran, their footfalls made puffs of dust rise in the air. Their armor was getting dirtier by the moment. The fine particles might cause system troubles if the Hish were not careful. At the very least, their equipment would need attention when the Hunt was over.

Mal-Rek suggested the use of a plasma burst to hobble the humans' vehicle. That way they could end this particular Hunt and return to the colony to track other prey. He estimated that there were hundreds of humans back there. If they were pried from hiding and allowed to scurry like rodents, the party could take its time in killing them.

Before Mal-Rek could elaborate, Bet-Karh rejected the idea. It sounded brutal for the sake of brutality, not a proper Hunt at all. Most of those "rodents" were going to be unarmed, after all, and therefore unworthy of the hunters' attentions.

But Mal-Rek pressed his point as he kept pace with Bet-Karh. The humans, he argued, were not worthy targets in any case. They were nothing like the prey the Hish had found on worlds like Dantur and Kassin. Less-than-worthy targets could be dispatched in any way possible.

If the humans were so unworthy, Bet-Karh countered, how was it that they had killed two of the Hish? And how was it that they had escaped entrapment in the mountains?

The humans had proven tenacious, ingenious—ideal prey for any clan. The intelligence the Hish had gathered on the subject of humans served only to support what Bet-Karh had seen with his own eyes. But then, he added, perhaps Mal-Rek's clan had never encountered humans before. Or had occasion to study them.

Mal-Rek didn't answer. The silence gave Bet-Karh a feeling of superiority—one that was especially satisfying in light of Mal-Rek's arrogance. But it gave him yet another reason to keep an eye on Mal-Rek, who had to be chafing under the lash of Bet-Karh's remark.

Suddenly, Mor-Jut stopped dead in his tracks, forcing Blay-Kral and Pran-Ser to break their strides to avoid him. A moment later, Mor-Jut pointed to something perhaps twenty degrees to the right of the humans' vehicle. Bet-Karh followed his clan-brother's gaze with his infrared visor and saw what Mor-Jut had discovered.

Heat signatures, made faint by distance but signatures nonetheless. Humans, he realized. And it seemed they were on foot.

There was no way to identify them invidually—not from so far away. But Bet-Karh had a feeling in his gut that they were the ones who had eluded him in the mountains. And now, for some reason he didn't understand, they were *returning* to the mountains.

Had they left something of value there? Perhaps, unlike the humans in the settlement, they had chosen to live there. The list of possibilities was endless.

Not that it really mattered.

What *did* matter was that all the humans who had defied them were going to be in the same place. The realization made Bet-Karh's kill-gland swell with anticipation. And if the killing frenzy was building in *him*, it would soon build in his companions as well.

It didn't take long. Blay-Kral wanted to run down the humans who were still on foot, and then go after the vehicle later. Mal-Rek said that it was a good idea.

Bet-Karh thought otherwise. Amplifying his voice through a system built into his helmet for that purpose, he declared that the humans—*all* of the humans—were to be tracked to the mountains. Only there would they have a chance to survive, making the Hunt a worthy one.

Mor-Jut and Wrak-Oto, despite their drives to kill, gave grudging agreement to their clan-mate. Mal-Rek, speaking for the other clan, agreed to the plan as well. However, the subtly rebellious tone in which he said it gave Bet-Karh fresh cause for concern.

He decided to overlook Mal-Rek's response. After all, they were in the midst of a Hunt. A satisfying chase and an equally satisfying ending would surely make the hunters forget their differences. It was only a matter of time.

The distance between the colony and the mountains was considerable. After a while, even Bet-Karh felt the strain of covering it. He wished he could strip off his armor, which wasn't made for such prolonged and repetitive activity and was becoming more uncomfortable by the minute.

All he could remove without stopping, however, was his helmet. He did this, feeling the night air cool on the flesh of his face. Seeing him, the others followed his example.

Bet-Karh bore the humans who were moving on foot a grudging respect. Especially their leader, the one who had piloted the digging machine. Its use was a stroke of ingenuity. Bet-Karh vowed that if he got the chance, he would confront that human and claim him as a trophy.

Soon, the mountains came to loom before them, large black silhouettes against the gray sky. To Bet-Karh's left were the shorter and less majestic shapes of the forest. The humans could have gone in that direction, but they had chosen otherwise.

It was understandable. The mining tunnels and natural formations provided far better hiding places and more defensible locations. It was where Bet-Karh would have taken his people were their positions reversed.

As he watched, he saw the humans in the vehicle move past the ones proceeding on foot, apparently failing to see them in the darkness. As a result, Bet-Karh had to make a choice. Either he could hunt one group first, leaving the other one for later, or split his hunting party and pursue both groups at once.

He decided on the latter strategy.

No doubt, Dre-Nath would have preferred him to mix each hunting group with members of both clans. After all, this was to have been an exercise in cooperation. However, he didn't believe he could keep Mal-Rek and Blay-Kral in check much longer.

Why not accept a limited victory with regard to cooperation and, at some point, let the malcontents go their own way—after one pack of humans or the other? Once they were in the mountains, only Mal-Rek and Blay-Kral would know how they hunted. If they wished, they could shame themselves and their clan. Bet-Karh would never know, and would therefore feel no need to correct the situation.

His own hunt, of course, would be conducted properly. With that in mind, he wished he could take Pran-Ser with him. He would show her how to hunt as Hish hunted in ancient times, and be present when she made her First Kill.

However, he believed Pran-Ser would wish to remain with her clan-mates. And if such was the case, he would not stand in her way.

Finally, about two miles shy of the mountains, Bet-Karh told the others what he had in mind. He, Mor-Jut, and Wrak-Oto would continue to pursue the humans who were on foot, whom—he said reasonably—were probably bone-tired and were therefore less worthy prey. Mal-Rek and the others would go after the humans in the vehicle, who were more rested and would therefore present more of a challenge.

As he might have expected, Mal-Rek resisted. He said that out of revenge for his brother's death, he wished to hunt the humans in the vehicle on his own. Bet-Karh, their glorious leader, could take everyone else and hunt the other humans.

Of course, that approach was unacceptable to Bet-Karh. Five hunters going after four humans? It was hardly worth the effort, and he said so.

He expected Mal-Rek to be obstinate, but he didn't expect the speed at which the argument escalated. When he looked back on the incident later, he would remember that each Hish had removed his or her helmet, and that the hormonal scents given off by their kill-glands amplified what each of them was already feeling.

The scents were like airborne pathogens. As the secretions rushed through the hunters' lungs and roiled through their bloodstreams, the hormones inflamed the animosity and clan rivalries that had existed previously. The result was unfortunate, but inevitable.

Blay-Kral was the first to raise his blades and point them at another Hish—Mor-Jut, who unhesitatingly extracted his own blades and brandished them in self-defense.

Blay-Kral rushed forward with an uppercut that Mor-Jut had apparently anticipated, because he was able to fend off the attack and counter with one of his own. The fight was on.

And not just between Blay-Kral and Mor-Jut. Suddenly, all the hunters' bodies were in motion.

Bet-Karh tried to place himself between Blay-Kral and Mor-Jut, but it was too late. There was green blood dripping from both their blades. And they were going at it undaunted, as if neither of them had been injured in the least.

Pran-Ser, the novice, had leaped headfirst into Wrak-Oto's midsection, sending the older female sprawling. As Bet-Karh watched, Wrak-Oto got to her feet in time to fend off the stripling's follow-up attack, but only barely.

Then Bet-Karh could watch no longer, for Mal-Rek was coming for him. Extending his blades, Bet-Karh staved off the other hunter's assault and launched one of his own. But none of his blows were intended to kill; he hoped to put an end to the melee before it went beyond the point of no return.

Unfortunately that point came all too quickly. When Pran-Ser went for Wrak-Oto again, Wrak-Oto used the stripling's momentum to toss her into Blay-Kral, sending the two of them to the ground. Seeing his chance, Mor-Jut leaped on Blay-Kral and drove his blades into the other hunter's chest.

Blay-Kral might yet have survived, his armor taking most of the punishment. But Pran-Ser, enraged by the ignominy of being used as a throwing weapon, activated her plasma emitter and took aim. Before Mor-Jut could react, the novice let loose a plasma bolt that ripped Mor-Jut apart.

Pran-Ser's aim was imperfect, however, and the burst hit Blay-Kral as well. By the time she realized her error, Blay-Kral's head had been torn from his shoulders.

For a moment, Pran-Ser just stood there, aghast at what she had done to her clan-mate. But her anguish ended when Wrak-Oto put her blades through the stripling's neck. Pulling them out, the older female watched the younger one collapse in a heap.

Seeing Mal-Rek launch himself at Wrak-Oto, Bet-Karh didn't think—he just reacted. Grabbing Mal-Rek from behind, Bet-Karh tried to keep the hunter from his revenge. But Mal-Rek wasn't easy to restrain. Striking the leader in the face with his elbow, he stunned Bet-Karh enough to slip out of Bet-Karh's grasp. Then, as Bet-Karh struggled to regain his senses, Mal-Rek engaged Wrak-Oto.

Clearly, Mal-Rek was stronger and more skilled than the female. He circled to his left and feinted, drawing a response from Wrak-Oto that left her woefully off-balance. Taking advantage of the opening, Mal-Rek struck and struck again, putting explosive power into each attack.

By the time Bet-Karh got to his feet, Mal-Rek had pierced Wrak-Oto's armor with his blades and was carving the life out of her.

Wrak-Oto shuddered once, then died. Withdrawing his blades, Mal-Rek threw Wrak-Oto's body aside as if it were mere refuse, and not the flesh that had housed the spirit of a hunter. Bet-Karh glared at Mal-Rek, flushed with anger. His kill-gland was pumping furiously.

But part of Bet-Karh, the part that still thought like a leader, knew the only battle that really mattered had already been lost.

NINETEEN

Mal-Rek seethed as he returned Bet-Karh's glare, ignoring the corpses that littered the ground around him.

Bet-Karh knew he would either kill Mal-Rek or be killed by him. After all that had happened, there was no other possible outcome. But he waited, breathing rapidly with the effects of the gland, to see what the other hunter would do.

Only then would he strike.

It was a pity. Together, he and Mal-Rek could still carry out the hunt. They could collect their trophies, return to their hidden shuttles, ascend to the mother ship, and ask forgiveness for their sins. Dre-Nath and Kirs-Giras would be angry, but in the end the hunters would be forgiven.

After all, the Hunt was everything. And it wouldn't be the first time Hish had murdered each other in the heat of the Hunt.

But Bet-Karh could not tolerate that outcome. Mal-Rek and his clan-mates had proven without the slightest doubt what Bet-Karh had known all along—in fact, what they had *all* known, from Dre-Nath and Kirs-Giras down to the least stripling: It was folly to try to fashion one clan out of two. They were too different from one another, too diametrically opposed in terms of their most basic philosophies, to coexist much less cooperate.

As if to underline that grim and costly lesson, Mal-Rek activated his plasma caster and took aim at Bet-Karh. The gun swiveled into position and flared to life. But it would be another half a second before the blast came.

Quickly, Bet-Karh estimated where Mal-Rek had aimed the weapon—his midsection, in this case—and resolved to be elsewhere when the energy burst arrived.

The red light on Mal-Rek's shoulder glowed brighter and shifted to white—just as Bet-Karh hurled himself at Mal-Rek's knees.

The plasma gun fired. As the single glowing bolt struck the ground instead of Bet-Karh, it kicked up a huge plume of dirt. And before Mal-Rek could adjust his aim, Bet-Karh took his legs out from under him.

Reaching for Mal-Rek's plasma caster, Bet-Karh began to twist its targeting servo-motors. Mal-Rek's fists beat against him like hammers, threatening to drive the breath out of his lungs. But Bet-Karh's armor absorbed enough of the impact for him to bend the metal of the motors and render Mal-Rek's plasma caster inoperable.

Switching tactics, Mal-Rek grabbed the back of Bet-Karh's unprotected head and used his forehead to butt the leader in the face. The force of the blow made Bet-Karh recoil, green blood spurting from his facial orifices. Taking advantage of the opening, Mal-Rek dealt him a vicious backhand, which sent Bet-Karh sprawling.

Getting his feet beneath him, Mal-Rek tried to leap onto Bet-Karh, but Bet-Karh rolled in the dirt and avoided him. Then Bet-Karh scrambled to his feet as well, eyeing his enemy across a space of less than six feet. As if at a signal, both hunters extended their blades.

No words were exchanged, no taunts, no threats. There was no need. Both combatants knew that this was a fight to the death.

Mal-Rek took the offensive, as was his nature, striking Bet-Karh with the heel of his foot. The force of the blow sent Bet-Karh staggering backward, which gave Mal-Rek the opportunity to surge forward and strike him again.

And again. As before Bet-Karh's armor took the brunt of the attack, but not all of it. He felt his legs turning rubbery from the savage and prolonged punishment.

He had to subdue Mal-Rek once and for all. And he had to do it quickly, before he reached the point where he could no longer defend himself.

Timing his move, he ducked Mal-Rek's next blow and opened his lower mandibles—so much so that they nicked his enemy's hands. That was enough to stop Mal-Rek's momentum. Then, so Mal-Rek couldn't strike him again, Bet-Karh wrapped him in a bear hug and tried to break his ribs.

But Mal-Rek got his arms around Bet-Karh as well, and squeezed as hard as he could. At that point, it became a question of who could exert the greater force. Bet-Karh was determined that it would be *him*.

But Mal-Rek was a powerful individual. Bet-Karh could feel his bones bending, his lungs being deprived of air. And still he squeezed, trying to make Mal-Rek suffer even more.

The stalemate went on for what seemed like forever, stretching from seconds to minutes. Finally, Mal-Rek's left leg sagged a bit under the strain. Encouraged, Bet-Karh pressed his advantage and slowly, bit by bit, felt his opponent's grip weaken.

But Bet-Karh was weakening too. It was time, he felt, for a change of tactics—something Mal-Rek wouldn't expect, considering his adversary seemed to have the upper hand. Without warning, Bet-Karh released his opponent and used one of his blades to slash at Mal-Rek's face.

One eye was sliced in half and the flesh around it was carved to the bone, causing blood to gush from the wound. With a second slash, Bet-Karh severed Mal-Rek's lower mandibles.

Mal-Rek screamed in pain and lashed out, attempting to disfigure Bet-Karh as Bet-Karh had disfigured him. But Bet-Karh deflected the attacks with infinite patience, and waited for his opening. Maimed as he was, Mal-Rek was still dangerous—too dangerous to be allowed to draw another breath.

Finally, Bet-Karh saw his chance. Ducking a wildly swung set of knives, he came up driving his blades into his adversary's throat. So powerful was the blow that it nearly severed Mal-Rek's head from his neck.

Bet-Karh saw the shadows of confusion and pain and loss fall across his enemy's face. Then Mal-Rek slumped against him, his body lifeless and inert.

Had this been a hunt, Bet-Karh would have celebrated his achievement. But it wasn't a hunt. It was murder.

Thrusting Mal-Rek's body from him, Bet-Karh watched it pump its life's blood onto the dirt, leaving a pool of green liquid. He had been anointed the leader of his hunting party but he had no one left to lead. He was a failure, no longer worthy of his designation.

Locating his helmet, he replaced it on his head. With practiced ease, he reattached the breathing tubes one by one. Then he considered the scattered bodies of his fellow hunters and asked himself what he should do with them.

He decided to find the shuttle that had transported him to the planet's surface, bring it there, and load the bodies for return to his people. Once he got them there, the proper ceremonies would be carried out.

But first, he had to find the humans and complete his work. He had told Dre-Nath that he would find out how the Hish were lured to this world. He had yet to make good on that promise.

He had taken perhaps a hundred steps in the direction of his hidden shuttle when Bet-Karh changed his mind. Before he did anything else, he had to contact Dre-Nath and beg for forgiveness. It would pain him to do so, but anything less would be unworthy.

He activated the communications array in his helment and once more attempted to reach the mother ship. But as before, all he received was static. Something was wrong, he sensed. *Very* wrong.

Dre-Nath always answered Bet-Karh's calls, without exception. If he failed to do so now, it was because he couldn't. And Bet-Karh didn't want to consider any situation in which Dre-Nath had been incapacitated.

Because that would have signified violence on the mother ship. Between clans, perhaps. Certainly, such a disaster had been building since the two clans became one.

And Bet-Karh couldn't escape the feeling that it had been his fault. After all, he was the chosen Hunt Leader. He was the one who had directed what took place on the planet's surface. He had to atone for what he had done somehow. He had to resurrect the Hunt, even if he had to hunt alone.

The first step, he decided, was to track down the leader of the walking humans, the one who had proven so elusive. He would find this one and kill him. Then he would carve a trophy from him and dedicate it to the Hish who had fallen.

The success of that Hunt would be just the barest beginning of his personal road to redemption. But it would be a beginning.

Turning his back on the corpses of those he had led, Bet-Karh took off at a lope in the direction of the mountains.

TWENTY

Andar felt like a failure.

Since early that morning, he and his companions had been on the run. They had watched their comrades die horrible deaths. They had gone without food, water, and rest. And even now, they remained targets for alien hunters.

All in all, thought Andar, it had been one hell of a crappy day.

The notion of returning to the mountains and their mine tunnels had seemed like the smartest move. It still did. If Andar could have saved the colony somehow, he would have done it. As it was, he was trying to save the people around him.

Of course, the mountains, which loomed before them now in the darkness, were hardly a perfect solution. They were devoid of warmth, food, and most everything else Andar and his companions needed. But for now, safety was more important than anything.

As they trudged through the starless night, Andar kept his ears open and tried to identify every sound he heard. No doubt, there were mammals and birds and reptiles that came out after dark, foraging for their meals. But they wouldn't make the kinds of sounds he was listening for.

Not that there would necessarily be any sounds. The aliens could be pretty quiet if they wanted to be. As big as they were, they should have made a lot of noise. But they were hunters. Apparently, they had gotten good at sneaking up on people.

"Hey," said Mara, catching up with Andar, "you were working back on Earth, right?"

Andar confirmed that it was so.

"I heard they were trying to resurrect the old big leagues," said the redhaired man. "Whatever happened with that?"

"Who cares?" asked Broadhurst, who had evidently overheard the exchange. His voice was thin and hoarse, but there was a note of animation in it. "After the fix of twenty-two, it wasn't baseball anymore."

Andar looked back over his shoulder at the lawyer. "You're a fan?"

"I was," said Broadhurst. "Till the Angels threw the series and things started going downhill."

"Yeah," said Mara. "That was a shame. But it was the eco-disasters that put the kibosh on it."

"On *everything*," Andar noted.

He hadn't been there to see Earth go into the dumper, but it was his job to help with the cleanup. So he knew a few things about the disasters that had halfway ruined the planet.

As before, they lapsed into silence. But Andar found himself grateful for the chatter. It was good for them, taking their minds off their situation and their fatigue.

Except for Emphalelo. He alone hadn't spoken, lost somewhere in his thoughts. Andar had never met a sensitive before. He had no idea what the man might be thinking.

Suddenly, he heard one of those sounds he had been listening for—but it wasn't a footfall. It was mechanical, low and thrumming. *A vehicle*, Andar thought. Not strong enough to start a vibration in the ground beneath their feet, but pretty close.

"Down," he hissed.

They all hit the ground and stayed there. Andar felt for his weapon and found it. Not that he thought it would help much, but it made him feel better to do something rather than nothing.

Fortunately, the sound began to fade almost immediately. In a few seconds it was gone, which was a huge relief. Whoever was in it hadn't detected them, it seemed. But they knew they weren't out of the woods. The vehicle might circle back if Andar and the others gave it a reason.

Mara put his hand on Andar's shoulder and leaned in close. "What if it's someone from the colony?"

It was a possibility. But Andar shook his head. "We can't take the chance."

Of course, he hadn't seen the aliens use any ground transportation. But that didn't mean they *wouldn't* under the right circumstances. Only that they hadn't.

Even more wary than before, they went on. And before long, they came to the mountains. But it wasn't easy to find a tunnel or cave entrance in the dark. Not nearly as easy as it had been during the day.

Finally, Emphalelo pointed to something. "Over there," he said.

Andar saw it—an L-shaped outcropping. Just beyond it was a black shape, signifying a hole of some sort.

"We need light," he said.

Before he could dig out his cellular, he heard the rustle of a hand in a pocket. A metallic click followed and a small light came alive—Mara's. As they got closer to the opening, he raised the device over his head.

"I'll check it out," said Mara.

It was a good idea. The fewer lights, the better. And if there was something dangerous in the cave, only Mara would be exposed to it.

Andar watched Mara's light go around the outcropping and disappear, swallowed by darkness. A minute or so went by. Then Mara emerged, still holding his light.

"This should do," he called back.

Andar led the way into the cave. Taking out his own cellular device and activating it, he could see that the cave was actually pretty big—a sort of cavern. There were stalactities as well as stalagmites, though not many of either. And the walls were rough, naturally formed as opposed to the result of mining activity—about the best thing they could have hoped for.

They could rest there, even sleep a bit. And they only had to guard the entrance—the cavern didn't seem to connect with the network of tunnels. Andar wanted to see if there were any mining tools around that he could use as weapons, but he could look for those in daylight.

"Good work," he told Emphalelo, who had spotted the cavern in the first place.

Emphalelo shrugged. "Just luck."

"I'll take it," said Andar.

Mara volunteered to stand first watch outside their refuge. No one argued. Andar found a flat place next to a relatively smooth section of wall, rested his back against it, and closed his eyes in the darkness.

He didn't think it would take him long to fall asleep. But he was wrong. Tired as he was, sleep was denied him.

He heard someone chuckle and turned to find a shadow sitting a couple of yards away. "Can't sleep either?" asked Broadhurst, identifiable only by his voice.

"I could use some hot cocoa," Andar quipped, surprised that he still had a rudimentary sense of humor. But then, Katarina had always liked that about him.

He had spoken to her only about a day earlier, and yet she seemed so distant. So far away, as if she belonged to some other reality. It saddened him to think so.

"I'll heat some up," said the lawyer, sounding as depleted as a man could be and still be alive.

210 FRIEDMAN AND GREENBERGER

Andar frowned. "I'm sorry. I really am."

"For what?" asked Broadhurst.

"For bringing you out here. If I knew there would be alien hunters gunning for us, I never would have considered it."

"I was coming anyway," said the lawyer. "It was my job. Had to be done." He paused. "Got a question for you."

"Shoot."

"What the hell is a rattlin' bog?"

Andar laughed, louder than he should have. He hoped he hadn't woken Emphalelo.

"It's just an old song," he said.

"Damned odd one," Broadhurst said.

"It's not the words I find appealing," said Andar. "It's the tempo. Something I heard as a kid that trickled back into my mind earlier and stuck there. Was I bothering you with it?"

"You, no. The repetition, yes."

A few moments later, Broadhurst started to drift off. It was evident from the change in his breathing.

Andar wasn't so lucky. Now the song was rolling around his head again . . .

And the bird in the nest,
And the nest on the twig,
And the twig on the branch,
And the branch on the tree,
And the tree in the bog,
And the bog down in the valley-o!

Before he knew it, there was brightness in his eyelids. Sunlight was streaming through the entrance and filling the cavern. The air was still cool, leading Andar to believe that he hadn't been sleeping for very long. A few hours, at best. He felt anything but rested.

He was hungry, too. And thirsty. And he ached all over, unaccustomed to this kind of activity.

Mara, he noted, was just inside the cave entrance, a pistol in his right hand. Had he stayed awake the whole time? They nodded to each other, the older man looking more composed despite his lack of rest.

But then, they hadn't been attacked in hours. It was more than they might have hoped.

Picking himself up, Andar crossed the cavern and joined Mara. "See anything?" he asked.

Mara shrugged. "Something flew by, but it was nothing." He smiled. "Good thing those bastards can't get airborne."

If they could, Andar and his companions would have been toast some time ago. "Good thing," Andar agreed. He glanced at Broadhurst and Emphalelo, who showed no signs of waking. "Let these two sleep. I'm going to stretch my legs and see if I can find us something to nibble on."

"I wouldn't go out there alone," Mara cautioned. "In fact, none of us should be solo until this is over."

"I appreciate that," said Andar, "but we need food. And I've really got to pee."

Mara considered it for a moment. Then he said, "Go. I'll keep an eye on you."

Emerging from the cave, Andar saw the sunlight gild the treetops of the forest, and lighten the sky from black to an angry purple. He could hear birds, if only just a chirp here and there.

Aware of Mara's scrutiny, and comforted by it, he nonetheless found a bush behind which to do his business. Then he looked around for something he could bring back—nuts, berries, whatever.

The hunger pangs that had gnawed at him through the night had faded for the moment, but he knew the hunger would be back with a vengeance. They would need food if they were to go on.

But he couldn't find anything that looked edible. And even if he did, he realized, he couldn't be sure it wasn't poisonous. Frustrated, he made his way back to the cavern.

Andar was so focused on the food problem, he failed to notice the shadows cast from the rocky outcropping near the cavern mouth. He did notice, however, that Mara was nowhere in sight. Rather than wake the others, he assumed Mara's position at the entrance.

If Mara didn't show up soon, Andar would have to go looking for him. But he had a feeling that Mara simply answered the call of nature, even as Andar himself did, and that he would be back momentarily.

He was still completing the thought when he saw a boot out of the corner of his eye, followed by an impact to the side of his head. It sent him reeling, staggering to one knee. Looking up, he saw Anton Kaganas smiling down at him from atop the outcropping. And he wasn't alone. Peter Jurgens was standing beside him.

Andar tried to get up, but Kaganas jumped down from the outcropping and kicked him a second time, knocking him flat.

"What the hell's going on?" Andar asked, hoping to wake the others—if they were still alive.

Kaganas answered by kicking him again, this time in the ribs. The breath knocked out of him, Andar fell onto his side and gasped for air.

Before he could pull himself together, Jurgens disarmed him and threw his gun away. Then he grabbed Andar by his shirt and dragged him up. Andar tried to twist free of the man's grasp, but Jurgens held onto him with a grip like steel.

"Your cousin wants you dead," Jurgens whispered in his ear, obviously deriving pleasure from the announcement.

His foul breath made Andar wince. But it confirmed what he had suspected—that Derek was behind it all, somehow.

Kaganas reached into one of his pockets and withdrew a knife—a vicious-looking thing—and pulled his arm back to bury his blade in Andar's neck. But before he could do what he intended, his arm was grabbed from behind.

Andar turned to see who his savior was—and saw Emphalelo struggling with the much bigger, stronger Kaganas. The dark-skinned man was yanking on Kaganas's wrist, trying to force it back further so he would drop the knife.

Andar took that opportunity to drive his heel into Jurgens's toes, eliciting a yelp of pain—and earning Andar a respite from Jurgens's grip. Slipping an arm free, Andar cracked his elbow into his captor's face. His nose smashed and bleeding, Jurgens took a step backward.

At the same time, he reached for his weapon. It was slate-gray, long barreled, and clearly well-maintained. If he could squeeze off a shot, there was no question the gun would obey.

But Andar wasn't about to let him do that. Whirling, he grabbed Jurgens's wrist and forced it upward, at the same time burying his knee in Jurgens's groin.

The man yowled, but managed to bring the butt of his gun down on Andar's head, staggering him. Then, before Andar could recover, his adversary backhanded him with the gun.

Andar felt himself going down, his knees unable to keep him upright. His vision was filling with black spots, and an ache in his head was all that kept him conscious.

Wiping away some of the blood on his face, Jurgens stood there as Andar collapsed. Then he trained his gun on his enemy. And smiled, obviously enjoying himself.

That's it, Andar thought. *All done . . .*

Suddenly, Jurgens cried out and clutched the back of his head. Almost at the same time, a fair-sized rock hit the ground, sending up a puff of dust. Even in his dazed state, Andar could piece together that the rock had caused Jurgens's discomfort.

Looking past his enemy, Andar saw who had thrown the thing. It was Broadhurst. He was bending down in the recesses of the tunnel to pick up another missile.

Cursing volubly, Jurgens turned to face his attacker. Broadhurst froze, seeing the gun trained on him. He would have perished then at Jurgens's hands, except Jurgens had forgotten about Andar—who, rousing himself from his daze, picked up the rock Broadhurst had thrown and used it to smash Jurgens in the head.

The blow ruined Jurgens's aim, sending his shot caroming around the cavern. A look of outrage on his face, Jurgens wheeled—and received another blow, this time to the jaw.

Had it just been Andar's fist, the impact might not have staggered him so. But the rock made a much more formidable weapon. Jurgens stumbled and fell, his gun going off harmlessly into the cloud-ridden sky.

Caught up in an irresistible wave of hatred and resentment, Andar leaped on top of Jurgens, straddled his chest, and used his knees to pin Jurgens's arms to the ground.

Then he hit the sonuvabitch again, and again, and again.

Andar wouldn't let up. The world around him was a haze. All he could see was Jurgens. Zeroing in on the broken nose, he swung the rock and made sweet contact.

Blood spurted anew. But this time, there was no scream of pain from Jurgens—just a moan. And Andar continued to punish him, continued to smash him with the rock.

All he could think about was what he and his comrades had endured, how they had survived, and how they were going to continue to survive despite everything. Derek's goons weren't going to stop them—not now, not ever.

No one was.

Andar kept on pounding the man beneath him until his hands were themselves bloody, the skin torn away from his knuckles. He was rearing back for another shot when something tugged at his arms. He looked up to see Owen Broadhurst's face looming over his.

The lawyer looked worried.

"What . . . ?" asked Andar, barely recognizing his voice. It came out more like a snarl than anything fashioned by a human throat.

"Enough," said Broadhurst.

Finally, Andar looked down and saw what had become of Jurgens. His face was a swollen, mangled mess, painted with a thick layer of blood. But what caught Andar's attention were the man's eyes. They were fixed and lifeless.

Lifeless . . .

Andar scrambled off the corpse, weak as he was, and looked down at it as if it were the work of someone else. His hands climbed to his face like small, pale animals, a veneer of blood— his as well as Jurgens's—making his skin glisten in the early morning light. Drops of gore fell from his fingers and mixed with the dirt beside the dead man's ear.

He coughed, and it almost knocked him over. "What have I done?" he rasped.

"What needed doing," Broadhurst said.

Andar glanced at him, then moved backward, trying to distance himself from the body. The lawyer kept pace with him, no doubt concerned that Andar would collapse.

"It was either him or you," said Broadhurst. "I could plead self-defense on your behalf and no one would argue the point."

"You don't understand," said Andar, unable to take his eyes off the body. "I left the family. I'm not like them." He swallowed back his horror. "I never wanted this."

"Of course not," Broadhurst said sympathetically.

"What have I become?" Andar asked numbly.

He hadn't intended it to be a real question, but he got a reply anyway: "A survivor."

Andar continued to stare at Jurgens's corpse until he felt Broadhurst's hand on his shoulder. "The others . . ." he said.

Mara. Emphalelo. They were still out there. The last Andar had seen of Emphalelo, the man was struggling with Kaganas—a fight he couldn't possibly win.

That thought forced Andar into action. Making his way out from the cavern mouth as best he could, he found Emphalelo lying face down on the ground. He had already accepted the man's death, adding it to the toll for which he felt responsible, before he saw Emphalelo stir.

"He's alive," said Broadhurst, evidently as surprised as Andar was.

Together, they knelt beside the sensitive and turned him over. He had sustained a bloody injury to his side—a knife wound from the look of it—but not a bad one. Something else must have laid him flat.

Andar shook him a little and his eyes came open. Obviously, he was in some pain.

"What happened?" asked Andar.

"Kaganas . . ." said Emphalelo, wincing at the pain it cost him to speak. "He stabbed me . . . but Mara shot him." He shook his head. "That's all I know."

Andar looked around. There was no sign of either Mara or Kaganas. Their confrontation must have taken them elsewhere.

Then Broadhurst pointed at something. "Look!"

Andar followed the gesture until he spotted two figures mostly hidden by the bend of the mountain. They were both bloodstained. Yet they were still striving against each other, feinting and slashing with the knives clutched in their fists.

Mara must have noticed the approach of his companions, because he held up a hand and called to them to stop. "Stay away," he said, "the bastard's mine!"

Ignoring the demand, Andar started forward anyway. But Broadhurst restrained him. "That's the way they are," he said, "when there's bad blood between them. They don't see it the way you and I do."

Shrugging Broadhurst off, Andar kept going—until it occurred to him that he would feel the same way about Derek. He would want the chance to kill the bastard on his own, just as he had killed Jurgens.

Except in Derek's case, he would enjoy it.

So he hung back and watched, however reluctantly. And as he did so, he saw Kaganas drive his blade into Mara's arm. It looked like the cut bit deep, slicing into muscle and tendon.

But Mara didn't cry out. Instead, he kicked at his attacker, pushing Kaganas back. It was clear, though, that Mara was having trouble moving his hand. Fortunately, he wielded his knife with his other one.

Kaganas charged him again, blade raised high, ready to sink it into his adversary. But Mara had other ideas. Turning sideways, he allowed Kaganas's momentum to send him to the dirt. Then, before Kaganas could recover, Mara buried his knife to the hilt between Kaganas's shoulder blades—unfortunately, more to the right than left and therefore away from the hitman's heart.

Unlike Mara, Kaganas screamed long and loud.

Mara stood there, swaying, unsteady, blood dripping freely down his arm and pooling at his feet. His enemy was still alive, though the steel in his back kept him from moving very much. Damaged as they were, neither of them made a move to go after the other.

Finally, Kaganas pushed himself off the ground into a sitting position, his knife in his right hand. Andar could see now that he was bleeding from a wound in his side as well, though it wasn't clear whether he had taken a blade or a bullet.

If Kaganas couldn't get up, it would be tough for him to defend himself. He must have known that. Mara must have known it too, because he was slowly moving closer to his adversary.

At last, grinning with grim determination, Mara drew his knife back and leaned in, preparing to execute the coup de gras. But Kaganas, who was more mobile than he had let on, switched his knife to his left hand and thrust upward, cutting Mara under his ribcage and into his organs. As Mara trembled, making a choking sound, Kaganas slashed to the right, tearing through Mara's abdomen. Blood spilled from the wound, followed by a coil of steaming, red intestine. Unable to complete his swing Mara collapsed, his knife finally tumbling from his lifeless fingers.

Kaganas let out a triumphant laugh, making Andar's jaw clench. Then he choked, coughed up blood, and fell backward into the dirt.

Andar and Broadhurst went to take a closer look. Both men were dead. Finding Mara's knife, Andar picked it up and brushed the dirt off it.

This is what it's come to, he thought. *No longer Predator versus human, but human versus human, Ciejek versus Ciejek.*

Derek was playing for all the marbles without realizing that as long as the Predators roamed freely on Felicity, he would never be able to take those marbles home. In fact, none of them were going home. That much was becoming clear.

"We need to see to Emphalelo," Broadhurst said in a weary voice.

Andar nodded and went back to the mouth of the cavern. "How did they find us?" he wondered out loud. "Those flying things?"

"I don't know," said the lawyer.

Andar also didn't understand why Derek's men had come after them when there were Predators in the area. He said so.

"Good question," said Broadhurst. But he didn't seem to have an answer.

Emphalelo hadn't moved since they left him. But he was more alert. Together, Andar and Broadhurst helped the man sit up.

"What happened?" asked Emphalelo.

"Mara's dead," said Andar. "Kaganas too."

Emphalelo's brow furrowed when he heard the news. "Mara saved my life. And it wasn't the first time."

"We should get back inside the cave," said Broadhurst.

Andar looked around in the rising light. He didn't see anyone, Predator or otherwise. But that didn't mean they weren't out there.

Together, he and Broadhurst hoisted Emphalelo to his feet, careful to avoid touching his wound. Then, with Emphalelo's arm slung over his neck, Andar helped the man back into the cavern.

In the process, they passed Jurgens. Disfigured as he was, he no longer looked real. He had been reduced to a bloody piece of meat, albeit a big one.

Once inside the cavern, they used strips of their clothing to bandage Emphalelo's wound. Afterward, they sat down and gathered their strength—what was left of it. Andar felt light-headed, ready to conk out. He needed food and water, and so did the others.

But he hadn't found any outside the cavern. Another search, he believed, would simply produce the same results. Then he remembered . . .

Jurgens. Kaganas. They might have been carrying some food or water. Especially if Derek had anticipated their being out there a while.

It was worth a shot. Dragging himself to his feet, Andar told his companions where he was going. Under different circumstances, Broadhurst would probably have talked him out of it. After all, Andar was spent.

But Emphalelo had lost a lot of blood. Without food and water, he might go into shock. So on this occasion, the lawyer said nothing.

As Andar emerged from the cave, the air already felt warmer than before. Soon, it would be hot out. He had to work as quickly as possible.

The idea of going through Jurgens's pockets repulsed him, but he forced himself to do it. He was rewarded with the discovery of a small water bottle and some candy bars.

Andar wanted to slosh the water down his throat and devour the bars. But he restrained himself, knowing Emphalelo needed them more than he did. Making sure that Jurgens didn't have anything else, he shoved his booty into his own pockets and moved on to Kaganas.

Unlike Jurgens, the bald-pated Kaganas hardly looked any different from when he was alive. He seemed to be on the verge of opening his eyes, even saying something. And yet, he didn't object when Andar rifled his pockets.

Again, Andar struck paydirt. Another half-full water bottle, more candy bars, even a strip of beef jerky. As much as Kaganas had loved scotch, Andar almost expected to find a flask as well.

Broadhurst and Emphalelo would be happy, he told himself, as he stuffed his pockets with the stuff. Getting to his feet, he fought off a wave of dizziness and started back toward the cavern.

It'll be cool there, Andar thought. *We can rest. Figure out our next move.*

When he passed Jurgens again, he didn't even glance at the man's corpse. He was already learning to live with what he had done.

As he entered the cool darkness of the cave, it took his eyes a moment to adjust. In that moment, he heard Broadhurst cry out.

Before Andar knew what was happening, he heard a crack— like a thick piece of ice breaking in half.

Broadhurst was sitting with his back to the cavern wall, a blank look in his eyes, a rivulet of blood making its way down his face from a dark spot in the middle of his forehead.

Turning to his left, Andar saw the source of the bullet that had killed his friend the lawyer. Even in the dimness of the cavern, he couldn't mistake the leering grin of his cousin.

"So good to see you," said Derek.

Andar didn't react right away. Slowly and ever so painfully, it came to him that Broadhurst's shout had been an attempt to warn him about Derek. And for his trouble, he had been murdered in cold blood.

"You should thank me," Derek said, following his cousin's gaze. "He was a pain in the ass."

The anger built up in Andar so suddenly, he found himself trembling. With an animal sound tearing from his throat, he charged across the cave and launched himself at his cousin.

But he never reached him. Derek's gun slammed into the side of his head, nearly causing him to lose consciousness. Before he knew it he was lying on the ground, the taste of blood in his mouth. And he was looking up at Derek.

His cousin still had a pistol in his hand, pointed at Andar's face.

"Son of a bitch," Andar snarled.

Derek smiled at him. "Not nice of you to speak of your Aunt Elaina that way."

Andar looked around the cavern for Emphalelo. The man was sitting with his back against one of the walls, his eyes closed. Was *he* dead too?

Andar turned back to his cousin. "Why did you do it?"

"What," Derek asked, "kill your men?"

"No, bring the Predators here."

Derek shrugged. "I have plans for the family business. You were going to shut it down, sell it off, or convert it into something less profitable. I couldn't allow that. The Predators were a way to take you out of the picture without implicating myself."

"But they'll destroy the entire colony."

"Unfortunate, I agree. But you know what they say about breaking eggs to make omelets."

Andar shook his head. "We're not talking about omelets, you idiot. We're talking about human beings. You've thrown us to the wolves—your men, my men, everybody on the planet. And for what? *Money?*"

"You know it's about more than that," said Derek. "It's power. It's about being what Grandpa Karl was—the boss."

"Big deal," Andar spat.

"If you didn't think so, why did you come back? Why didn't you stay on Earth where you belonged?"

"I would have, except I knew what would happen to my father's men."

"So you came back to protect them?" Derek glanced at Broadhurst, and then at Emphalelo. "Nice job."

Andar managed a smile as cold as his cousin's. "You too. Or did you miss seeing Jurgens on the way in?"

For just a moment, Derek's anger showed. Then he stifled it. "So now it's just you and me. And Marlene—but she's back in our ground vehicle, getting her beauty sleep."

"Don't forget the Predators," said Andar.

"How can I?" Derek asked reasonably. "They blew up my shuttle."

"So how are you going to survive? Can you find a way off Felicity before the aliens make a trophy out of you?"

Derek frowned. "That's one mess I haven't figured out yet. But don't worry, I will." He leveled his gun at Andar's chest.

"Sorry, but it's time to say goodbye. Since you're family, I'll make it quick."

"Family?" Andar spat. "After what you did to my father?"

Derek lowered his gun, his eyes widening in surprise. "How did you know about that?

"Your drones. They were seen the day my father died."

Derek's expression changed to one of understanding. "Yeah, the drones. Hey, when I start a job, I make certain it gets finished." He chuckled, remembering. "He was finally beginning to think you had a point with all your crap. He was talking about changing our business, getting out of some parts and getting into others. That wasn't the way I saw it."

"So you killed him."

"He was an impediment. He had to go." Derek raised the gun again. "Just like you."

Andar braced himself for the impact. But before his cousin could squeeze the trigger, they heard a noise—the scrape of a boot on the rough, uneven ground at the entrance to the cavern. More quickly than Andar would have imagined, Derek whirled and fired.

It was only as the echoes of the shot reverberated that either Andar or his cousin realized whom Derek had killed.

Marlene stood there for a moment clutching her sternum, an expression of surprise on her face, blood trickling from between her fingers. Then she spun around and hit the ground.

"Marlene . . . ?" said Derek, as shaken as Andar had ever seen him.

Seeming to forget about his cousin for a moment, Derek pelted across the cavern and sank to his knees beside Marlene. Andre had never imagined that Derek cared that much about the woman, but he saw then that he was wrong.

He took advantage of the distraction to move closer to his cousin. But he hadn't gotten more than halfway when Derek looked up, his eyes red-rimmed and angry.

"You little shit," he said, his voice thick with emotion. "I was going to let you off easy. Now you're going to die slow." And, easing Marlene to the ground, he leveled his gun again at Andar—this time aiming low, maybe at his cousin's kneecaps.

"That's far enough," came a voice, strained and colorless.

Andar looked to the source of it and saw Emphalelo, lying on his side with a gun in his hand. He didn't look like he could do much with it, but he was a threat Derek couldn't ignore.

As Derek whirled to address it, Andar capitalized on the last chance he was likely to get. Taking two strides, he flung himself across the intervening distance. As Derek's shot rang out, Andar plowed into his cousin's knees as hard as he could.

Together, they fell in a mess of arms and legs. Andar clawed at Derek's weapon, battling him for control of it. For a second or two they struggled, both of them jockeying for position. Then Derek lost his grip and the gun went clattering across the cave floor, well out of reach.

Derek went for it anyway. As Andar grabbed him, he got an elbow in his face. Still, he hung on, weighing Derek down. Derek strove to push his cousin away, to slither out of his grasp.

But Andar wouldn't let it happen. Grabbing hold of Derek's belt, he pulled himself forward and drove his fist into his cousin's jaw. Snarling with rage, Derek struck back.

They fought like their earliest ancestors, bodies in desperate, furious motion, all action and reaction. Andar punched, tore, gouged, fueled strictly by rage, doing whatever he could to gain the upper hand.

He felt his right eye puff up, obscuring some of his vision. His mouth was full of blood. Breathing had become a challenge, each intake causing him a sharp pain in his side—no doubt a cracked rib.

And still he fought.

After a while, he sensed that Derek was tiring, but no more than Andar himself. His arms felt like lead, nearly impossible to lift. His breath came in hot, searing gasps, like daggers in his side. When he struck, his blows had no force behind them.

Finally, marshaling one last surge of energy, Andar drove his fist into his cousin's face. Groaning, Derek went limp. Knowing he had bought himself a chance, Andar got up, staggered across the cavern, and retrieved Derek's gun.

Then, breathing like a bellows, his vision blurry on one side, he returned to his cousin and stood over him. Derek turned his head and looked up at Andar, his face swollen and bloody. Somehow, he looked like a little boy again, awash in pain and frustration.

Just the way Andar remembered him.

But Derek wasn't a little boy anymore. He was a killer, cold and methodical. He had murdered Andar's father, and Laban, and Broadhurst, and maybe in the end the entire colony.

Andar aimed the gun at Derek. Could he kill his own flesh and blood? Could he?

Derek spat blood and propped himself up into a sitting position. "So this is it," he managed to say between deep, racking breaths.

Andar nodded, though he was still uncertain. "Looks like it."

Derek's head tilted appraisingly to one side. "You won't do it. We both know that. You're a bleeding heart. You've got no balls."

Andar winced as sweat stung his battered eye. "That's an interesting way to beg for your life."

"Why should I?" Derek chortled. "You're too weak to kill me. And the longer you wait . . ." He pushed himself up on one knee, " . . . the more likely it is that I'll kill *you*."

Andar's jaw clenched. *Do it*, he told himself. *Don't be an asshole.*

What was the difference? He had already killed Jurgens. What was one more death on his hands?

Especially for a Ciejek.

Andar aimed the gun at a spot on Derek's soiled, torn shirt, beneath which he thought he would find his cousin's cold, shriveled heart. *Do it*, he insisted.

He was still trying when he saw three red dots materialize in the same spot.

TWENTY-ONE

Bet-Karh hadn't gone far toward the base of the mountains before he heard the sounds of a fight. Had he failed to hear them, he would have had a difficult time tracking down the leader of the humans. As it was, the humans had made his task simplicity itself.

But as he approached the spot from which the sounds had come, his cloak active, he wondered why the humans were shooting at each other rather than at the Hish. Were they too the victims of conflicts across clans? His curiosity spurred him to greater speed.

Bet-Karh was glad for the distraction. Anything to take his mind off the situation on the mother ship, which promised to be a disheartening one. After leaving Mal-Rek's corpse, he had tried repeatedly to raise Dre-Nath. However, his every attempt had met with frustration, adding to his misgivings.

Was it possible that his brethren were all dead? That they had destroyed each other out of stubborn loyalty to their separate clans—just as he and Mal-Rek had attempted to destroy each other?

If he was right, and he was the sole survivor, then his options were limited. A hunter without a clan was a cipher, a loose end. After all, how could one hunt on one's own, without a ship to cross the stars in search of new hunting grounds? How could one find prey?

Hish subjected to such a fate often went insane, or else took their own lives. Or they faded away, never to be heard from again.

Of course, Bet-Karh could pilot the mother ship on his own, if his warring brethren hadn't damaged it too severely. Then he could find the prey he craved. But it would be a solitary existence all by himself on the big, echoing starship, and therefore a painful one.

His acquisition of one last trophy—the skeleton of the human leader—wouldn't do much to assuage that pain. But he was a hunter, and he had to do *something*.

He found the humans' hideout in even less time than he would have imagined. Just outside the hideout, there was a human corpse, and not far away, a couple of humans were engaged in combat. There was bloodshed, killing, of which naturally Bet-Karh approved.

A moment after Bet-Karh's arrival, two more humans appeared. However, they didn't join the battle. They merely watched, allowing the combatants to continue on their own.

Bet-Karh took note of the gesture. Were the humans afraid of getting involved? Or were they showing respect to the combatants? It was difficult to tell.

Then he recognized one of the humans hanging back. His features were bloodied and swollen, but it was the leader—the one Bet-Karh had decided to hunt. If the hunter wanted to, he could have finished off the human then and there.

But it seemed an unworthy act to kill prey while it was distracted by something else. And more so if he had caught the human in the act of showing respect to others.

Bet-Karh considered the situation, and decided not to consummate his hunt. He could kill the human leader any time he chose to do so. Better to wait and examine the circumstances more closely than to do something he would later regret.

So he stood and watched, unseen. Soon, the combat drew to a close. One human killed the other, though his wounds were grievous and they claimed him a few breaths later.

That left the human leader and his companion. Together, they returned to a half-hidden cavern, in the process picking up a third human who seemed to be part of their clan.

Then the leader went out again, apparently to relieve the corpses of their supplies. It made sense. When resources were scarce, it was necessary to secure them by any means possible. Bet-Karh noticed with interest that the leader did not make use of the food and drink he obtained. Obviously, he was saving them for his companions. A decision worthy of a leader.

Remaining invisible, the hunter followed the human back to the cavern. But when they arrived, there was a newcomer—a human with a weapon in his hand, which he had just used to kill another human.

The leader attacked the newcomer, but the newcomer was armed. The leader and the newcomer exchanged words. A great deal of them, it seemed to Bet-Karh.

He wished he had a translator program since humans spoke so often and at such length. Few among his people desired to know how their targets thought or communicated, feeling that the knowledge muddied the waters of their own thinking.

All Bet-Karh could do was try to understand the humans through their body language. That provided ample data for him to get the gist of what they were saying.

Finally, the newcomer seemed ready to kill the leader. However, the leader didn't ask for mercy. His tone was a belligerent one, as befit his status.

Just then, a female entered the cavern, and the newcomer killed her instead of the leader. Bet-Karh didn't understand the newcomer's motivation. He understood it even less when the newcomer went to the female's side and embraced her.

Was he insane?

As the newcomer mourned the female, the leader edged closer to his enemy. However, it didn't appear he would get close enough, until the other human in the cavern—one who was badly wounded—grabbed a weapon and drew the newcomer's attention.

That gave the leader a chance to close the gap. Flinging himself on the newcomer, he grappled with him for the weapon. In the course of their struggle, the gun was thrown across the cavern floor.

Still, the two humans continued to fight. Finally, tired and injured, the leader obtained the advantage and acquired the weapon. Then he stood over his adversary and trained the weapon on him.

Bet-Karh expected that the confrontation would end then and there. But it didn't. The leader hesitated.

The hunter wondered why. The newcomer was all but helpless. He had killed one of the leader's comrades and attempted to kill another. But something held him back.

Not fear, certainly. Not physical disability. Something else.

To Bet-Karh's mind, it could be only one thing: a code of conduct. The Hish had them. Apparently, humans did as well.

However, the newcomer had killed a member if his own clan—the female. He seemed to regret it, but that didn't change the fact that he had done it. He deserved to die.

Perhaps the leader couldn't kill him, for reasons Bet-Karh didn't understand. But the hunter wasn't hampered by any such restriction.

Switching off his cloak, he activated the targeting mechanism on his plasma caster and took aim at the newcomer's chest. Then he fired, and a white-hot plasma bolt flew across the cavern.

At the last moment, the newcomer moved—and spoiled Bet-Karh's aim. Instead of punching a hole in his chest, the bolt tore his head off.

The leader turned to Bet-Karh and stared, open-mouthed. Neither of them tried to communicate. They just stared, their eyes locked.

Bet-Karh had promised himself that he would kill this one. He had made it his goal, his only goal.

However, the human had displayed qualities worthy of a Hunter. He had demonstrated ingenuity in protecting his companions. He had fought hard against an armed adversary and won. And he had cared for another of his kind even when it was to his detriment.

Bet-Karh lowered himself from his observation post and took up a position on the hard ground, the human gaping at him all the while—no doubt wondering what he would do.

It was a good question, since Bet-Karh didn't know himself.

Andar had no idea how far he could get against a Predator. Its armor repelled bullets as well as energy blasts. Knives were useless against it. And his own two hands were too sore and too ineffectual to do anything but pray for his life.

When Derek's head exploded, Andar was covered in blood, brains, and gore. With the backs of his useless hands, he wiped away as much as he could off his face, hoping none of it had gotten into his mouth.

Derek's death took all the hate out of him, and hate was all he had been going on. His efforts to survive had taken their toll the last twenty-four hours. He was a mass of aches and injuries, tired beyond belief.

At his best, he would have been no match for the monster in front of him. As it was, he was less than that.

But the Predator, fresh from his destruction of Andar's cousin, was slowly clambering down from its perch. Andar knew better than to run. *Let me die with some dignity*, he thought, and stayed where he was.

Besides, he wanted to take a look at one of the hunters who had caused him so much pain and misery. If it was true that the Predators lived to hunt, they had done their share of it on Felicity.

Fascinated, Andar watched the alien touch the floor of the cavern and unfold itself to its full height. It was huge, at least seven feet tall, and it looked powerful beneath its armor. And its plasma emitter was active, judging by the red light glaring from it.

It seemed the Predator was studying him too, its eyes moving up and down his frame. But the alien's knives never came out from its wrists, and his plasma gun didn't fire. In fact, the brute made no move against him at all.

Should I try to communicate with it? he wondered.

Was this a chance for a positive contact with the hunter species? Could he and the Predator even find a common ground for communication, or were their thoughts and customs too alien to each other?

Before Andar could choose, the alien made the choice for him. Without warning, it turned its back on him and walked away in the direction of the cave mouth.

Andar didn't know why it had decided to leave him alone, when it had killed so many other human beings. However, it occurred to him that the wisest course would be to stay where he was until the Predator was well out of sight.

Only then did Andar breathe a sigh of relief and make his way to Emphalelo. Fortunately, Derek's shot had gone awry, because the sensitive was still alive. What's more, he held the gun he had obtained, if only loosely.

"Thanks," said Andar, kneeling beside the wounded man.

"No problem," said Emphalelo, his voice thin and weak.

Andar looked around for the water containers he had salvaged, and found them near the entrance to the cavern. Recovering them, he propped Emphalelo up and trickled some water down his throat. Almost immediately, the man gained a little strength.

Then he took out a candy bar, stripped the wrapper off, and gave it to Emphalelo. The man devoured it. And a second one, almost as quickly. Only after Emphalelo insisted did Andar consider having some water and part of a candy bar himself.

"I need a doctor," Emphalelo said apologetically.

"I'll get you one," Andar promised him.

After all, Derek had mentioned a ground vehicle—the one in which he had left Marlene. All Andar had to do was find it, get Emphalelo inside it, and take it back to the colony. There would be physicians there, and he would find one.

Of course, the colony residents would still be hiding from the Predators. But somehow, he had a feeling that the aliens wouldn't be a threat. Maybe it was the way that one Predator had looked at him, or the fact that it had spared his life. He couldn't say. But his instincts told him that the aliens wouldn't be a problem any longer.

If that were true, Andar had just one problem in front of him—settling the family business. There wouldn't be any legalities to deal with, not anymore. He was the sole surviving descendant of Grandpa Karl, and it all belonged to him.

But he wouldn't take the family business as it was. He would remake it as he saw fit. He would use the infrastructure that had exploited Earth and its people to help heal the planet. It wouldn't happen overnight, obviously, but he could at least get the ball rolling.

Emphalelo's eyes narrowed. "You've changed," he said.

Andar nodded. "I know."

As he got to his feet, he felt the fear and terror drain from his body, and his mind returned to saner thoughts—like Katarina. It was the best decision of his life not to let her join him in this madness. There was so much he wanted to tell her, about his plans, dreams, hopes . . . even his suspicions as to what a "rattlin' bog" might be.

By then, the Predator had been gone from sight for several minutes, and Andar felt safe enough to go looking for Derek's ground vehicle. Putting one leaden foot ahead of the other, he left the cave.

Jurgens's body was still there by the entrance. Andar vowed to have it collected, along with the bodies of everyone else who had worked for the Ciejeks, and returned to their families. It would be the first undertaking of his grandfather's newly reformed business.

He couldn't wait.

EPILOGUE

Walking back through the forest to his shuttle, Bet-Karh despaired for his people. The universe was getting crowded. They were no longer the only species capable of spanning the stars.

The humans were everywhere, it seemed, popping up on world after world. Short of an all-out war, he doubted the Hish could exterminate all of them—even if war were the way of Bet-Karh's people.

And there might be other species, to that point unknown to the Hish. Species that might be as clever as the humans, or even more so. Species that might be as powerful as the Hish.

Bet-Karh's people were going to have to adapt. And so was he.

The first step, he knew, was to restore honor to his clan, even if he was the last member of it. It would take time. Years, probably. But he had time.

This Hunt had taught him much, but there were some lessons he wished he had learned sooner. For instance, that there can be only one leader. Or that clans must remain separate from one another. Or that a hunting ground may not be what it seems.

He had to make certain others learned faster than he did. Perhaps that would be his role from that point on—to educate his people. To impart his experiences to those in need of such knowledge.

The destiny of the Hish might depend upon it.

AUTHOR'S NOTE

A collaboration only works when the two writers involved are comfortable with one another, each one willing to put aside his ego and throw out a beloved character or plot twist because his partner has come up with something different—maybe better, maybe worse, but it's something that partner believes in.

We have worked together on numerous occasions (sometimes just the two of us, sometimes with others) and reached that point long ago. Which, given the circumstances, made writing this book a lot easier than it might have been.

People often wonder how these things work. The flip answer is usually, "I wrote the vowels, he wrote the consonants," or "I wrote the good parts, he wrote the rest." The reality is a little more complicated.

Editor Rob Simpson and Mike had worked together on a couple of other books—*Aliens: Original Sin* and *The Wolf Man: Hunter's Moon* (still in print, buy them now)—when Rob suggested that Mike write a Predator novel. This sounded like a nice challenge and Mike accepted it. But looking at his calendar, he knew he couldn't comfortably handle the project without some help. That was when he turned to Bob, who could be counted on to help keep things moving.

Mike wrote a two-page pitch for Twentieth Century Fox's approval and then Bob expanded it into a chapter-by-chapter outline. Mike massaged that into something with a bit more detail; Bob took it and got to work. As Bob first-drafted each chapter, he would send it off to Mike, who would polish and expand it. Bob would then review the revised material, making a tweak or two. When the book was finished, Mike gave it a final spit polish, making it shine. Then it went off to Dark Horse Books.

But not to Rob, because by then Victoria Blake had taken over the Alien and Predator franchises at Dark Horse. After Victoria edited the manuscript and received Twentieth Century Fox's comments, Mike went back in to make the requisite adjustments.

Which brings us to the work you hold in your hands. We hope it lived up to your expectations.

Neither of us could have done the work in the time allowed without the love, patience, understanding, and support of our families. In Mike's case, we're talking about his long-suffering wife Joan and his younger son Drew, who gave him the space he needed and threw him a slab of raw meat now and then. His elder son Brett was away at college, but Mike felt the vibes from Carlisle as Brett cheered him on.

Bob, whose kids are *both* away at college, was able to count on his wife Deb to share the trials and tribulations of the project, and he appreciated having Dixie the Wonder Dog keep him company, lying at his feet as Bob pounded away at the keyboard.

We were and are appreciative of Rob's and Victoria's insights, support, and guidance as the book lurched from concept to finished manuscript. Thanks, guys. Couldn't have done it without you.

—Mike & Bob